P9-DWM-749

CALGARY PUBLIC LIBRARY

SEP   2014

SLOW COOKER

DOUBLE DINNERS
FOR TWO

SLOW COOKER

DOUBLE DINNERS
FOR TWO

Cook Once, Eat Twice!

Cynthia Graubart

Photographs by Rick McKee

GIBBS SMITH
TO ENRICH AND INSPIRE HUMANKIND

First Edition
18 17 16 15 14   5 4 3 2 1

Text © 2014 by Cynthia Graubart
Photographs © 2014 by Rick McKee

All rights reserved. No part of this book may be reproduced by
any means whatsoever without written permission from the
publisher, except brief portions quoted for purpose of review.

Published by
Gibbs Smith
P.O. Box 667
Layton, Utah 84041

1.800.835.4993 orders
www.gibbs-smith.com

Printed and bound in Hong Kong
Cover design by Sheryl Dickert
Gibbs Smith books are printed on paper produced from
sustainable PEFC-certified forest/controlled wood source.
Learn more at www.pefc.org.

Library of Congress Cataloging-in-Publication Data

Graubart, Cynthia Stevens.
  Slow cooker double dinners for two / Cynthia Graubart ;
photographs by Rick McKee. — First edition.
      pages cm
  Includes index.
  ISBN 978-1-4236-3625-0
1. Electric cooking, Slow. 2. Cooking for two. I. Title.
  TX827.G76 2014
  641.5'884—dc23
                    2013034618

CONTENTS

INTRODUCTION

The Rival brand Crock-pot in avocado green, circa 1970, was the slow cooker I grew up with. It was the appliance that revolutionized my mother's kitchen as she raised two children while working and attending college. Having dinner ready and waiting was a boon to her then, and has remained so for me even today.

This countertop treasure has been there as an extra pot to hold side dishes warm for parties, has made dinner while I carpooled to baseball games and ballet lessons, and now provides portion-friendly dinners for just my husband and me.

I truly enjoy what I call "recreational cooking"—when I have music playing in the background, my favorite retro apron tied on my waist, and lots of pots and pans simmering, boiling, roasting, and baking, with my thoughts on the friends and family that will gather at my table to share these dishes made with love.

What I find most challenging in the kitchen is putting a regular meal on the table night after night. While raising my family, I was a master at meal planning and always knew what we were having for dinner. Now with my nest empty, I've felt a little lost.

One of the biggest transitions from cooking for my family to cooking for two has occurred at the grocery store. Those "family packs" of chicken thighs still cackle their siren call toward me from the meat case, and I must say I find it difficult to resist. But honestly, why do I need ten chicken thighs? Even "regular"-sized packages serve at least four people!

That's when I realized that I could still purchase the regular pack, but instead of making a full recipe of a dish that would yield leftovers, I could do two different preparations, yielding two completely different flavors. Using slow cooker liner bags as cooking bags, I could separate the two recipes to keep them from commingling in the crock and thus produce what I'm calling **Double Dinners**. Now you can cook two different meals in the same slow cooker at the same time, yielding one dinner for tonight and a second meal for another night this week, or wrap it to freeze for another time. Cook once, eat twice! Now there's a real time-saver!

So now you see why I think that every cook passes through one phase or another where a slow cooker can be a lifesaver—or at least a sanity-saver! Whether you are a newlywed, an empty nester, living in a small apartment, or cook in a place where the slow cooker might be the only appliance available (vacation cabin, boat, or RV), this book is for you.

The recipes do not call for browning or other additional preparation steps requiring another appliance such and a stove, oven or microwave. Each recipe is designed for two, with a little left over for lunch or perhaps a second light meal or a third drop-in diner. All of the ingredients can be found in your local grocery store, without an extra trip to a specialty store.

SLOW COOKER SAFETY

Read the manufacturer's guide that came with your slow cooker. It contains information unique to your appliance. Never use an extension cord to plug in a slow cooker. The cord is purposefully short to prevent the appliance from accidentally tipping over.

The outside of a slow cooker gets hot, so keep it away from children and pets, low-hanging cabinets, and walls.

Do not wash a slow cooker insert until it has cooled *or the pot might crack*.

HOW TO USE THIS BOOK

First, obtain the slow cooker liner bags. They are essential to the success of the recipes. At the present time, Reynolds brand is the most widely available, usually found on the same grocery aisle as plastic bags and aluminum foil. Regency Wraps, Inc., also makes liner bags, found online or at some specialty retailers. Reynolds and Regency liners are BPA-free and approved by the FDA for cooking.

The recipes have been created in pairs (A's and B's) to make it easy on the cook. Each pair calls for a common package size of chicken, beef, lamb, or pork to split between two liner bags. Each A and B will have separate preparation directions, and at the end of recipe B will be the cooking directions for cooking both bags in the same slow cooker.

I've tested all of these recipes in my Cuisinart $3^{1}/_{2}$-quart slow cooker. A 4-quart slow cooker is also a good size here. For a variety of slow cooker recipes for two, including everything from the classic pot roasts, to Cornish hen, to side dishes of potato gratin and ratatouille, see my previous book, *Slow Cooking for Two: Basics, Techniques, Recipes* (Gibbs Smith, 2013).

WHY SLOW COOKING?

Slow cooking is an ideal cooking method to tenderize tough cuts of meat. It's also a boon to the busy cook who could benefit from a recipe that cooks unattended. A slow cooker uses about the same amount of electricity as a 75-watt bulb.

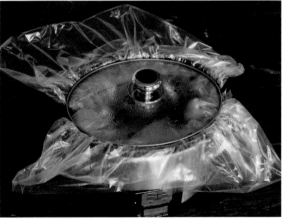

ABOUT SLOW COOKERS
SELECTING A SLOW COOKER

Slow cookers are available in many sizes, from just 1-quart all the way up to 7-quart. For a typical family, a 5- to 7-quart size is ideal, but it's too large when cooking for two. I've found the best size for me is the $3\frac{1}{2}$-quart slow cooker. There are a few choices in that size range; I like one with these handy features:

- High, Low, Warm, and Off settings
- Programmable Timer
- Auto switch to Warm at the end of cooking time
- Power indicator light
- See-through lid
- Removable crock
- Oval shape (more accommodating to irregular-shaped foods)

IMPORTANT RECIPE TIPS

A common complaint about slow cooker recipes is that they all taste the same or look the same. While it's true that what a slow cooker does best is the long, slow braise, which usually means a beef roast is involved, there are ingredients to further jazz up your recipes. At the end of cooking, stir in any of the following:

- Additional chopped fresh herbs
- Grated lemon or lime rind
- A little extra garlic
- A dash of soy sauce, sriracha, pesto, or other ready-made sauce
- A dollop of tomato paste
- A bit of chopped cooked bacon
- A little extra grated cheese, usually Parmesan
- Seasonings to taste, especially more salt and pepper

Don't lift the lid during cooking unless directed by the recipe, or you'll need to add 20 minutes to the cooking time.

Dense root vegetables, like potatoes, cook more slowly than meat in the slow cooker, so put them in the cooker first, on the bottom and closest to the heat.

Don't fill slow cookers to the top. They cook most efficiently when they are half to three-quarters full.

COOKING TIMES

Different slow cookers vary in their temperature range. Most reach a temperature of 300 degrees on High, and 200 degrees on Low. Some cook fast (at a higher temperature) and some cook slow (at a lower temperature). You'll have to adjust cooking times to the quirks of your slow cooker. This can be a little frustrating at first, so allow some flexibility in the finishing time of a recipe the first time you make it—it might be ready a little earlier—or a bit later—than expected. Once you know how your slow

cooker operates, you'll be able to adjust the recipe cooking times accordingly.

Read the recipe all the way through before cooking, and assemble all ingredients. If you are transporting your dish to serve at a different location, plan to use a liner so you can tie the liner closed before transporting the meal in the slow cooker, thus precluding a nasty spill.

FAVORITE NON-SLOW COOKER RECIPES

Here's a handy chart for converting your non-slow cooker recipes.

CONVENTIONAL RECIPE TIME	SLOW COOKER TIME ON LOW
15 minutes	1½ to 2 hours
20 minutes	2 to 3 hours
30 minutes	3 to 4 hours
45 minutes	5 to 6 hours
60 minutes	6 to 8 hours
90 minutes	8 to 9 hours
2 hours	9 to 10 hours

A recipe that is normally braised on the stove or in the oven is a good candidate for the slow cooker.

FREQUENTLY ASKED QUESTIONS

DO I HAVE TO CHECK ON THE SLOW COOKER WHILE IT'S COOKING?

The first time you use your slow cooker, plan to be home. That way you'll be there to notice any quirks of your appliance. After that, you can leave the slow cooker to do the work alone.

DO I HAVE TO STIR?

Luckily, stirring is not necessary during cooking, unless specifically indicated in the recipe. In fact, lifting the lid to stir when it's not indicated will increase the cooking time by 20 minutes.

DOES THE SLOW COOKER STOP AUTOMATICALLY?

Only if you have a programmable machine, which I highly recommend. Otherwise, set a timer so you can be ready to turn your slow cooker to WARM or OFF.

WHAT IF I OVERCOOK THE RECIPE?

A slow cooker is very forgiving. Usually the cooking times are for a range of time, so not to worry. The recipes in this book will specify if there is a danger of overcooking.

HOW LONG CAN A RECIPE SIT IN THE SLOW COOKER?

The programmable slow cookers are set to turn automatically to the WARM setting after cooking. They then switch to OFF after 2 hours. As a general rule, food should not sit for more than 2 hours after cooking, or there is an increased risk of bacteria growing.

CAN I CONVERT MY OWN RECIPES TO THE SLOW COOKER?

Yes, but primarily they should be recipes based on long, slow cooking on the stove or in the oven, with liquid to help create steam. See the rough conversion chart on the facing page.

CAN I BAKE IN MY SLOW COOKER?

Yes! Check out the cake and bread recipes in my book *Slow Cooking for Two: Basics, Techniques, Recipes.* Experiment to come up with new recipes.

CAN I MIX AND MATCH THESE RECIPES?

Absolutely! You can cook chicken next to pork, or any combination you desire. The only consideration is that the two dishes need to cook at the same temperature and time.

CAN I DOUBLE JUST ONE RECIPE?

That's a great idea. For example, if you want to prepare the whole chuck roast (both halves), follow the recipe for your favorite version and double everything EXCEPT the liquid—add only 50 percent more. For instance, if the recipe calls for 1 cup of broth, when doubling add just 1½ cups broth, not 2 cups.

THE SLOW COOKER PANTRY

I'm a firm believer in a well-stocked pantry. It's especially handy when life gets in the way of my plans. The recipes in this book are based on pantry staples, ensuring you'll have the ingredients on hand.

REFRIGERATOR

- **Dairy**—butter, milk, half-and-half or heavy cream, and a variety of cheeses (blocks to freshly grate, or already grated or shredded). Parmigiano-Reggiano is the king of all Parmesan cheese, and its extraordinary taste is well worth the extra expense.

- **Vegetables**—a variety of fresh herbs (basil, chives, cilantro, oregano, parsley, rosemary, tarragon, thyme), carrots, celery, bell peppers, hot peppers, eggplant, ginger, kale, spinach, leeks, lemons, limes, mushrooms, zucchini

- **Condiments**—ketchup, Worcestershire sauce, soy sauce, Dijon and spicy brown mustard, hoisin sauce, favorite hot sauce, salsa, horseradish

- **Fully-cooked bacon**

DRY PANTRY

- Garlic, shallots, and onions
- Russet, red, new, and sweet potatoes
- Canned tomatoes in a variety of preparations—whole, crushed, diced, tomato sauce
- Marinated artichoke hearts
- Dried fruits and tomatoes
- Flour (all-purpose and self-rising), cornstarch, and/or quick-cooking tapioca for thickening sauces
- Brown and white sugars, honey
- Breadcrumbs
- Broths—chicken, beef, vegetable
- Red and white wine, dry sherry, port
- Vinegars—white, red wine, balsamic
- Oils—olive oil, other cooking oil
- Chipotle chile in adobo, canned green chiles
- Uncooked converted rice
- Dried lentils
- Canned black beans, cannellini beans, kidney beans
- Peanut butter
- Nuts—almonds, pecans, walnuts
- Capers, olives

- Jams and jellies
- Spices—allspice, bay leaf, chili powder, Chinese five-spice powder, ground cinnamon, ground cloves, ground coriander, ground cumin, Italian seasoning, ground nutmeg, ground sage, red pepper flakes

FREEZER

- Vegetables—corn, chopped onion, herbs
- Meats—flank steak, chuck roast, sirloin tip, bottom round, eye of the round, short ribs, pork tenderloin, beef and lamb stew meat, pork tenderloin, pork chops
- Poultry—boneless, skinless chicken breasts; skinless chicken thighs; boneless, skinless chicken thighs; turkey tenderloins

POULTRY

Chicken shows its versatility in virtually all cooking methods, and it certainly shines when cooked in a slow cooker. All the various chicken parts are enhanced with the low and slow method. My personal favorites are the chicken thighs, but you'll enjoy choosing from the variety here.

A. CHICKEN WITH ZUCCHINI AND MUSHROOMS
SERVES 2

Such humble ingredients yield such a delicious dish! Feel free to leave the mushrooms sliced, or chop if you prefer. In an effort to add more healthy grains to our diet, I serve this dish over red quinoa.

4 bone-in, skinless chicken thighs
Salt and freshly ground black pepper, to taste
1 teaspoon Italian seasoning
1/3 cup shredded or grated Parmesan cheese, divided
4 ounces sliced fresh mushrooms
1 small zucchini, sliced
1/3 cup chicken broth

1. Insert liner into the slow cooker, fully opening the bag and draping the excess over the sides.

2. Add chicken to the bottom of the liner. Season with salt, pepper, and Italian seasoning.

3. Sprinkle chicken with 3 tablespoons Parmesan cheese.

4. Reserve remaining Parmesan cheese to top finished dish for serving.

5. Top chicken with mushrooms and zucchini.

6. Pour chicken broth over chicken and vegetables.

7. Fold the top of the bag over to one side and push ingredients at bottom of liner over to create room for the second bag.

8. Follow directions for the second recipe.

continued >

B. CHICKEN WITH SWEET POTATOES AND FIGS
SERVES 2

Sweet potatoes and figs taste like fall, and when the first tease of cooler weather arrives, this is the first dish I serve.

4 bone-in, skinless chicken thighs
Salt and freshly ground black pepper, to taste
1/3 cup chopped dried figs
1 small sweet potato, peeled and diced
1 small onion, diced
1/2 cup chicken broth
1/4 cup orange juice
1/2 teaspoon ground ginger
1/2 teaspoon ground coriander
1/2 teaspoon ground turmeric
1 teaspoon ground cumin
Dash of cayenne pepper, optional

1. Insert liner into the remaining space in the slow cooker, fully opening the bag and draping the excess over the sides.

2. Add chicken to the bottom of the liner. Season with salt and pepper.

3. Top chicken with figs, sweet potato, and onion.

4. Stir together chicken broth, orange juice, ginger, coriander, turmeric, cumin, and cayenne pepper, if desired, in a small bowl. Pour over chicken and vegetables.

5. Fold the top of the bag over to the opposite side of the first bag and nestle the ingredients of both bags so that they are sharing the space evenly.

TO COMPLETE THE RECIPES:

1. Each closed liner should be draping away from the other, extending over the sides of the slow cooker.

2. Cover and cook on LOW for 5 hours.

3. Move two shallow serving dishes or bowls next to the slow cooker. Remove cover and using pot holders or oven mitts, carefully open each liner and remove the solids with a slotted spoon or tongs to its own serving bowl. Still using a pot holder, gather the top of the first liner, carefully lift the bag from the slow cooker and move over its serving bowl. Cut a corner off the bottom of the bag, large enough to allow the remaining contents of the bag to be released into the bowl. Discard the liner. Repeat with the second liner.

4. Allow the recipe not being served to cool, and package in a resealable plastic freezer bag or freezer container. Label and freeze up to 3 months.

5. Before serving, taste, and season again with salt and pepper. Top the Chicken with Zucchini and Mushrooms with reserved Parmesan before serving.

A. SOUTHWEST CHICKEN AND WHITE BEAN CHILI

SERVES 2

These tender chicken thighs have a little South of the Border flair.

4 bone-in, skinless chicken thighs
Salt and freshly ground black pepper, to
    taste
1 small red onion, chopped
1 (15-ounce) can cannellini beans, rinsed and
    drained
1 (10-ounce) can diced tomatoes with green
    chiles
2 cloves garlic, minced, or 1 teaspoon bottled
    minced garlic
1 teaspoon ground cumin
$1/2$ teaspoon chili powder
$1/4$ cup shredded cheddar cheese, optional
$1/4$ cup chopped fresh parsley, or to taste,
    optional

1. Insert liner into the slow cooker, fully opening the bag and draping the excess over the sides.

2. Add chicken to the bottom of the liner. Season with salt and pepper.

3. Top chicken with onion and beans.

4. Stir together diced tomatoes, garlic, cumin, and chili powder in a small bowl. Pour over chicken and beans.

5. Reserve cheese and parsley to top finished dish before serving, if desired.

6. Fold the top of the bag over to one side and push ingredients at bottom of liner over to create room for the second bag.

7. Follow directions for the second recipe.

continued >

B. CHICKEN WITH PARSNIPS AND APPLES
SERVES 2

This is a real homey dish. The parsnips are natural partners for the apples. I prefer a tart apple like Granny Smith in this dish. Serve with a tricolor couscous or a broccoli slaw.

4 bone-in, skinless chicken thighs
Salt and freshly ground black pepper, to taste
1 teaspoon chopped fresh rosemary, or ¹/₂ teaspoon dried rosemary
1 parsnip, peeled and finely chopped
10 baby carrots, finely chopped
1 small Granny Smith apple, peeled and finely chopped
1 small onion, finely chopped
1 teaspoon cider vinegar
¹/₄ cup chicken broth

1. Insert liner into the remaining space in the slow cooker, fully opening the bag and draping the excess over the sides.

2. Add chicken to the bottom of the liner. Season with salt, pepper, and rosemary.

3. Top chicken with parsnip, carrots, apple, and onion.

4. Add cider vinegar to broth and pour over chicken and vegetables.

5. Fold the top of the bag over to the opposite side of the first bag and nestle the ingredients of both bags so that they are sharing the space evenly.

TO COMPLETE THE RECIPES:

1. Each closed liner should be draping away from the other, extending over the sides of the slow cooker.

2. Cover and cook on LOW for 5 hours.

3. Move two shallow serving dishes or bowls next to the slow cooker. Remove cover and using pot holders or oven mitts, carefully open each liner and remove the solids with a slotted spoon or tongs to its own serving bowl. Still using a pot holder, gather the top of the first liner, carefully lift the bag from the slow cooker and move over its serving bowl. Cut a corner off the bottom of the bag, large enough to allow the remaining contents of the bag to be released into the bowl. Discard the liner. Repeat with the second liner.

4. Allow the recipe not being served to cool, and package in a resealable plastic freezer bag or freezer container. Label and freeze up to 3 months.

5. Before serving, taste, and season again with salt and pepper. Top Southwest Chicken and White Bean Chili with reserved cheese and parsley before serving.

A. RUSTIC MEXICAN STEW

SERVES 2

Homey and rustic with Mexican flavors, this dish will have you reaching for tortillas or tortilla chips. Serve with salsa or hot sauce as desired.

$\frac{1}{2}$ small (2-pound) package boneless, skinless chicken thighs, cut into chunks
Salt and freshly ground black pepper, to taste
1 (14$\frac{1}{2}$-ounce) can diced tomatoes, drained
2 teaspoons ground cumin
4 cloves garlic, minced, or 2 teaspoons bottled minced garlic
2 green onions, sliced, white and green parts, divided
10 baby carrots, sliced
$\frac{1}{2}$ cup frozen corn kernels
1 jalapeno pepper, seeded and finely chopped
Lime juice
2 tablespoons chopped fresh cilantro, or to taste
Salsa or hot sauce, as desired

1. Insert liner into the slow cooker, fully opening the bag and draping the excess over the sides.

2. Add chicken to the bottom of the liner. Season with salt and pepper.

3. Stir together tomatoes, cumin, garlic, white part of green onion, carrots, corn, and jalapeno in a medium bowl. Pour over chicken.

4. Reserve green onion tops, lime juice, cilantro, and salsa, if using, to top finished dish for serving.

5. Fold the top of the bag over to one side and push ingredients at bottom of liner over to create room for the second bag.

6. Follow directions for the second recipe.

continued >

B. CHICKEN CURRY WITH RED POTATOES
SERVES 2

Serve an Indian flatbread such as naan with this smoky-flavored dish. There's a great sauce for dipping.

½ small (2-pound) package boneless, skinless chicken thighs, cut into 1-inch pieces
Salt and freshly ground black pepper, to taste
1 small onion, diced
¼ teaspoon ground cloves
½ teaspoon ground ginger
¼ teaspoon ground nutmeg
½ teaspoon ground allspice
½ teaspoons curry powder
1 clove garlic, minced, or ½ teaspoon bottled minced garlic
1 jalapeno pepper, seeded and chopped
¼ cup coconut milk
¼ pound red potatoes, cut into ½-inch cubes

1. Insert liner into the remaining space in the slow cooker, fully opening the bag and draping the excess over the sides.

2. Add chicken to the bottom of the liner. Season with salt and pepper.

3. Top chicken with onion.

4. Stir together cloves, ginger, nutmeg, allspice, curry powder, garlic, jalapeno, and coconut milk in a large bowl. Add potatoes, stirring well to mix. Pour over chicken.

5. Fold the top of the bag over to the opposite side of the first bag and nestle the ingredients of both bags so that they are sharing the space evenly.

TO COMPLETE THE RECIPES:

1. Each closed liner should be draping away from the other, extending over the sides of the slow cooker.

2. Cover and cook on HIGH for 4 hours.

3. Move two shallow serving dishes or bowls next to the slow cooker. Remove cover and using pot holders or oven mitts, carefully open each liner and remove the solids with a slotted spoon or tongs to its own serving bowl. Still using a pot holder, gather the top of the first liner, carefully lift the bag from the slow cooker and move over its serving bowl. Cut a corner off the bottom of the bag, large enough to allow the remaining contents of the bag to be released into the bowl. Discard the liner. Repeat with the second liner.

4. Allow the recipe not being served to cool, and package in a resealable plastic freezer bag or freezer container. Label and freeze up to 3 months.

5. Before serving, taste, and season again with salt and pepper. Top the Rustic Mexican Stew with reserved green onion tops, lime juice, and cilantro before serving.

A. CURRIED CHICKEN STEW

SERVES 2

This curry dish using dark meat, as in chicken thighs and legs, contains a little more calories than breast meat, but also more nutrition. Chicken thighs have myoglobin, which packs a punch in the iron department, and more zinc and B vitamins than chicken breasts.

1 medium white potato, peeled and diced
$\frac{1}{2}$ green bell pepper, cored, seeded, and cut into strips
4 bone-in, skinless chicken thighs
Salt and freshly ground black pepper, to taste
1 small onion, sliced
1 teaspoon ground coriander
$\frac{1}{4}$ teaspoon ground cinnamon
1 teaspoon sweet paprika
1 teaspoon ground turmeric
$\frac{1}{2}$ teaspoon crushed red pepper flakes, divided
1 teaspoon freshly grated ginger, or $\frac{1}{2}$ teaspoon ground ginger
1 (14$\frac{1}{2}$-ounce) can diced tomatoes, drained

1. Insert liner into the slow cooker, fully opening the bag and draping the excess over the sides.

2. Add potato and bell pepper to the bottom of the liner.

3. Top vegetables with the chicken thighs. Season with salt and pepper.

4. Top chicken with onion slices.

5. Stir together the coriander, ground cinnamon, paprika, turmeric, and $\frac{1}{4}$ teaspoon pepper flakes in a small bowl. Sprinkle over onions.

6. Reserve the remaining pepper flakes for topping finished dish before serving.

7. Stir the ginger into the diced tomatoes and pour over the chicken and vegetables.

8. Fold the top of the bag over to one side and push ingredients at bottom of liner over to create room for the second bag.

9. Follow directions for the second recipe.

continued >

B. JERK CHICKEN AND SWEET POTATO STEW

SERVES 2

Jerk seasoning gives these chicken thighs a spicy, exotic flavor. If you like cilantro, don't skip adding it to the finished dish.

1 medium sweet potato, peeled and diced

4 bone-in, skinless chicken thighs

Salt and freshly ground black pepper, to taste

2 cloves garlic, minced, or 1 teaspoon bottled minced garlic

1 tablespoon jerk seasoning

1 (14½-ounce) can diced tomatoes, undrained

3 tablespoons chopped fresh cilantro

1. Insert liner into the remaining space in the slow cooker, fully opening the bag and draping the excess over the sides.

2. Add sweet potato to the bottom of the liner and cover with chicken. Season with salt and pepper.

3. Stir the garlic and jerk seasoning into the tomatoes and pour over chicken.

4. Reserve cilantro to top finished dish for serving.

5. Fold the top of the bag over to the opposite side of the first bag and nestle the ingredients of both bags so that they are sharing the space evenly.

TO COMPLETE THE RECIPES:

1. Each closed liner should be draping away from the other, extending over the sides of the slow cooker.

2. Cover and cook on LOW for 5 hours.

3. Move two shallow serving dishes or bowls next to the slow cooker. Remove cover and using pot holders or oven mitts, carefully open each liner and remove the solids with a slotted spoon or tongs to its own serving bowl. Still using a pot holder, gather the top of the first liner, carefully lift the bag from the slow cooker and move over its serving bowl. Cut a corner off the bottom of the bag, large enough to allow the remaining contents of the bag to be released into the bowl. Discard the liner. Repeat with the second liner.

4. Allow the recipe not being served to cool, and package in a resealable plastic freezer bag or freezer container. Label and freeze up to 3 months.

5. Before serving, taste, and season again with salt and pepper. Top Curried Chicken Stew with remaining pepper flakes. Top the Jerk Chicken and Sweet Potato Stew with reserved cilantro before serving.

A. CHICKEN AND OLIVES

SERVES 2

More flavorful than chicken breasts, these chicken thighs soak up the Mediterranean influences of the olives and capers. Follow your preference about the hot sauce. Rice is a good side dish with this entrée.

4 bone-in, skinless chicken thighs
Salt and freshly ground black pepper, to taste
1 small onion, chopped
12 pitted green olives
2 tablespoons capers, rinsed and drained
¼ cup white wine
1 teaspoon Dijon mustard
¼ cup chicken broth
Dash of hot sauce, optional
¼ cup chopped fresh parsley, or to taste

1. Insert liner into the slow cooker, fully opening the bag and draping the excess over the sides.

2. Add chicken to the bottom of the liner. Season with salt and pepper.

3. Top chicken with onion, olives, and capers.

4. Stir together wine, mustard, and broth in a small bowl. Add a dash of hot sauce, if desired. Pour over chicken and vegetables.

5. Reserve parsley to top finished dish for serving.

6. Fold the top of the bag over to one side and push ingredients at bottom of liner over to create room for the second bag.

7. Follow directions for the second recipe.

continued >

B. PROSCIUTTO-WRAPPED CHICKEN
SERVES 2

Prosciutto is thinly sliced dry-cured ham, and the world's best comes from Italy. Now with purveyors in the United States, prosciutto is available much closer to home. This simple dish served over wild rice makes a lovely presentation. The sage leaves are key, so do sliver some to top the finished dish.

4 bone-in, skinless chicken thighs
4 slices prosciutto
1/2 cup chicken broth
1 teaspoon capers, rinsed and drained
4 fresh sage leaves, plus more for serving,
   optional

1. Insert liner into the remaining space in the slow cooker, fully opening the bag and draping the excess over the sides.

2. Wrap each chicken thigh with one slice of prosciutto. Add to the bottom of the liner.

3. Pour chicken broth over chicken. Sprinkle capers over all, and top each thigh with a sage leaf.

4. Reserve extra sage leaves, if desired, to top finished dish for serving.

5. Fold the top of the bag over to the opposite side of the first bag and nestle the ingredients of both bags so that they are sharing the space evenly.

TO COMPLETE THE RECIPES:

1. Each closed liner should be draping away from the other, extending over the sides of the slow cooker.

2. Cover and cook on HIGH for 3 hours.

3. Move two shallow serving dishes or bowls next to the slow cooker. Remove cover and using pot holders or oven mitts, carefully open each liner and remove the solids with a slotted spoon or tongs to its own serving bowl. Still using a pot holder, gather the top of the first liner, carefully lift the bag from the slow cooker and move over its serving bowl. Cut a corner off the bottom of the bag, large enough to allow the remaining contents of the bag to be released into the bowl. Discard the liner. Repeat with the second liner.

4. Allow the recipe not being served to cool, and package in a resealable plastic freezer bag or freezer container. Label and freeze up to 3 months.

5. Before serving, taste, and season again with salt and pepper. Top the Chicken and Olives with reserved parsley before serving. Top the Prosciutto-Wrapped Chicken with the reserved sage before serving.

A. ITALIAN-STYLE CHICKEN THIGHS

SERVES 2

The liquid from the diced tomatoes is all that's needed to render these chicken thighs moist and flavorful. If you haven't tried black rice yet, try it with this recipe; it's a super-healthy grain.

4 bone-in, skinless chicken thighs
Salt and freshly ground black pepper, to taste
1 (14½-ounce) can diced tomatoes
2 tablespoons tomato paste
2 cloves garlic, minced, or 1 teaspoon bottled minced garlic
2 teaspoons chopped fresh basil
¼ cup chopped fresh Italian parsley, or to taste

1. Insert liner into the slow cooker, fully opening the bag and draping the excess over the sides.

2. Add chicken to the bottom of the liner. Season with salt and pepper.

3. Stir together tomatoes, tomato paste, garlic, and basil in a small bowl. Pour over chicken.

4. Reserve parsley to top finished dish for serving.

5. Fold the top of the bag over to one side and push ingredients at bottom of liner over to create room for the second bag.

6. Follow directions for the second recipe.

B. BARBECUE CHICKEN THIGHS
SERVES 2

Barbecue the easy way, by doctoring up your favorite sauce and letting the slow cooker do all the work for you!

4 bone-in, skinless chicken thighs
Salt and freshly ground black pepper, to
   taste
$1/2$ cup favorite barbecue sauce
1 teaspoon Dijon mustard
1 teaspoon Worcestershire sauce
Dash of hot sauce, optional

1. Insert liner into the remaining space in the slow cooker, fully opening the bag and draping the excess over the sides.

2. Add chicken to the bottom of the liner. Season with salt and pepper.

3. Stir together barbecue sauce, mustard, Worcestershire sauce, and dash of hot sauce, if desired, in a small bowl. Pour over chicken.

4. Fold the top of the bag over to the opposite side of the first bag and nestle the ingredients of both bags so that they are sharing the space evenly.

TO COMPLETE THE RECIPES:

1. Each closed liner should be draping away from the other, extending over the sides of the slow cooker.

2. Cover and cook on LOW for 4 hours.

3. Move two shallow serving dishes or bowls next to the slow cooker. Remove cover and using pot holders or oven mitts, carefully open each liner and remove the solids with a slotted spoon or tongs to its own serving bowl. Still using a pot holder, gather the top of the first liner, carefully lift the bag from the slow cooker and move over its serving bowl. Cut a corner

off the bottom of the bag, large enough to allow the remaining contents of the bag to be released into the bowl. Discard the liner. Repeat with the second liner.

4. Allow the recipe not being served to cool, and package in a resealable plastic freezer bag or freezer container. Label and freeze up to 3 months.

5. Before serving, taste, and season again with salt and pepper. Top the Italian-style Chicken Thighs with reserved parsley before serving.

A. CHICKEN PROVENÇAL

SERVES 2

This chicken dish produces the perfect broth for sopping up with bread. Herbes de Provence is an herb mixture combing rosemary, sage, thyme, and sometimes lavender.

---

4 boneless, skinless chicken thighs
Salt and freshly ground black pepper, to taste
4 cloves garlic, minced, or 2 teaspoons bottled minced garlic
1 teaspoon herbes de Provence
$1/2$ red bell pepper, cored, seeded, and chopped
2 ripe plum tomatoes, diced
$1/4$ cup niçoise olives, pitted, or other small black olives
1 small orange
1 tablespoon Dijon mustard
$1/4$ cup white wine, or chicken broth
2 tablespoons chopped fresh parsley, or to taste

1. Insert liner into the slow cooker, fully opening the bag and draping the excess over the sides.

2. Add chicken to the bottom of the liner. Season with salt, pepper, garlic, and herbes de Provence.

3. Top chicken with bell pepper, tomatoes, and olives.

4. Zest the skin from about half of the orange and add to slow cooker. Juice the orange over a strainer, adding the juice to the slow cooker and discarding the leavings in the strainer.

5. Dissolve the mustard into the wine in a small bowl and pour over all ingredients.

6. Reserve parsley to top finished dish for serving.

7. Fold the top of the bag over to one side and push ingredients at bottom of liner over to create room for the second bag.

8. Follow directions for the second recipe.

continued >

B. BASQUE CHICKEN STEW
SERVES 2

Thyme is a tiny-leafed herb with a mild and distinct flavor; it is actually a member of the mint family. I love it in chicken and fish dishes. The leaves are easily stripped off of the woody stem with just your fingers.

4 boneless, skinless chicken thighs
Salt and freshly ground black pepper, to taste
4 sprigs fresh thyme, or $1/2$ teaspoon dried thyme
2 cloves garlic, minced, or $1/2$ teaspoon bottled minced garlic
2 small red potatoes, diced
1 small onion, diced
$1/2$ red bell pepper, cored, seeded, and thinly sliced
1 bay leaf
1 (14$1/2$ounce) can diced tomatoes, drained
$1/4$ cup shredded or grated Parmesan cheese

1. Insert liner into the remaining space in the slow cooker, fully opening the bag and draping the excess over the sides.

2. Add chicken to the bottom of the liner. Season with salt, pepper, thyme, and garlic.

3. Add potatoes, onion, bell pepper, bay leaf, and tomatoes.

4. Reserve Parmesan cheese to top finished dish for serving.

5. Fold the top of the bag over to the opposite side of the first bag and nestle the ingredients of both bags so that they are sharing the space evenly.

TO COMPLETE THE RECIPES:

1. Each closed liner should be draping away from the other, extending over the sides of the slow cooker.

2. Cover and cook on LOW for 5 hours.

3. Move two shallow serving dishes or bowls next to the slow cooker. Remove cover and using pot holders or oven mitts, carefully open each liner and remove the solids with a slotted spoon or tongs to its own serving bowl. Still using a pot holder, gather the top of the first liner, carefully lift the bag from the slow cooker and move over its serving bowl. Cut a corner off the bottom of the bag, large enough to allow the remaining contents of the bag to be released into the bowl. Discard the liner. Repeat with the second liner.

4. Allow the recipe not being served to cool, and package in a resealable plastic freezer bag or freezer container. Label and freeze up to 3 months.

5. Before serving, taste, and season again with salt and pepper. Top the Chicken Provençal with the reserved parsley before serving. Remove bay leaf and top the Basque Chicken Stew with reserved Parmesan before serving.

A. CHICKEN WITH MUSHROOM WINE SAUCE

SERVES 2

My husband calls this dish his slow-cooker *coq au vin*. For the reserved basil, stack the leaves on top of each other and roll tightly. Cut horizontally across the roll. You now have "chiffonade" of basil for topping.

½ small (2-pound) package boneless, skinless chicken thighs

Salt and freshly ground black pepper, to taste

1 small onion, chopped

1 clove garlic, minced, or ½ teaspoon bottled minced garlic

4 ounces sliced fresh mushrooms

¼ cup red wine

2 tablespoons tomato paste

2 teaspoons chopped fresh basil, plus additional leaves for serving

1. Insert liner into the slow cooker, fully opening the bag and draping the excess over the sides.

2. Add chicken to the bottom of the liner. Season with salt and pepper.

3. Top chicken with onion, garlic, and mushrooms.

4. Stir together wine, tomato paste, and basil in a small bowl. Pour over chicken.

5. Reserve basil leaves to top finished dish for serving.

6. Fold the top of the bag over to one side and push ingredients at bottom of liner over to create room for the second bag.

7. Follow directions for the second recipe.

continued >

B. BOK CHOY CHICKEN
SERVES 2

I love the milder flavor of baby bok choy, which is part of the cabbage family. Cut off the toughest part of the core at the bottom of the vegetable, then cut into horizontal slice and chop both the stems and leaves into 1-inch pieces.

3 small heads baby bok choy, chopped
1/2 small (2-pound) package boneless, skinless chicken thighs
Salt and freshly ground black pepper, to taste
1/4 cup tahini paste
1 tablespoon fresh lemon juice
2 teaspoons freshly grated ginger
1/2 teaspoon ground turmeric
2 teaspoons chopped fresh cilantro
2 green onions, sliced, white and green parts

1. Insert liner into the remaining space in the slow cooker, fully opening the bag and draping the excess over the sides.

2. Add bok choy to the bottom of the liner. Top with chicken thighs and season with salt and pepper.

3. Stir together tahini, lemon juice, ginger, turmeric, and cilantro in a small bowl. Pour over chicken.

4. Reserve green onions to top finished dish for serving.

5. Fold the top of the bag over to the opposite side of the first bag and nestle the ingredients of both bags so that they are sharing the space evenly.

TO COMPLETE THE RECIPES:

1. Each closed liner should be draping away from the other, extending over the sides of the slow cooker.

2. Cover and cook on LOW for 5 hours.

3. Move two shallow serving dishes or bowls next to the slow cooker. Remove cover and using pot holders or oven mitts, carefully open each liner and remove the solids with a slotted spoon or tongs to its own serving bowl. Still using a pot holder, gather the top of the first liner, carefully lift the bag from the slow cooker and move over its serving bowl. Cut a corner off the bottom of the bag, large enough to allow the

remaining contents of the bag to be released into the bowl. Discard the liner. Repeat with the second liner.

4. Allow the recipe not being served to cool, and package in a resealable plastic freezer bag or freezer container. Label and freeze up to 3 months.

5. Before serving, taste, and season again with salt and pepper. Top the Chicken with Mushroom Wine Sauce with reserved basil leaves, tearing if desired, before serving. Top the Bok Choy Chicken with the reserved green onions before serving.

A. INDIAN CHICKEN STEW
SERVES 2

This fruity stew is slightly sweet, but not heavy, and filled with flavor. Pine nuts are the seeds of pine trees found inside the pine cones. They have a slightly buttery flavor. Substitute your favorite nut as desired.

½ small (2-pound) package boneless, skinless chicken thighs, cut into chunks
Salt and freshly ground black pepper, to taste
1 small onion, sliced
10 baby carrots, sliced
¼ cup raisins
¼ cup dried apricots, chopped
½ cup chicken broth
1 tablespoon tomato paste
1 tablespoon lemon juice
½ teaspoon ground cinnamon
1 teaspoon ground cumin
1 teaspoon ground ginger
2 cloves garlic, minced, or 1 teaspoon bottled minced garlic
2 tablespoons pine nuts

1. Insert liner into the slow cooker, fully opening the bag and draping the excess over the sides.

2. Add chicken to the bottom of the liner. Season with salt and pepper.

3. Top chicken with onion, carrots, raisins, and apricots.

4. Stir together chicken broth, tomato paste, lemon juice, cinnamon, cumin, ginger, and garlic in a small bowl. Pour mixture over chicken.

5. Reserve pine nuts to top finished dish for serving.

6. Fold the top of the bag over to one side and push ingredients at bottom of liner over to create room for the second bag.

7. Follow directions for the second recipe.

continued >

B. CHICKEN STEW
SERVES 2

This colorful dish has a little kick but not overwhelming.

½ small (2-pound) package boneless, skinless chicken thighs, cut into chunks
Salt and freshly ground black pepper, to taste
1 small sweet potato, peeled and cut into small dice
½ cup frozen corn kernels
½ green bell pepper, cored, seeded, and sliced
¼ teaspoon cayenne pepper
1 (14½-ounce) can diced tomatoes

1. Insert liner into the remaining space in the slow cooker, fully opening the bag and draping the excess over the sides.

2. Add chicken to the bottom of the liner. Season with salt and pepper.

3. Stir together potato, corn, bell pepper, cayenne, and tomatoes in a small bowl. Pour over chicken.

4. Fold the top of the bag over to the opposite side of the first bag and nestle the ingredients of both bags so that they are sharing the space evenly.

TO COMPLETE THE RECIPES:

1. Each closed liner should be draping away from the other, extending over the sides of the slow cooker.

2. Cover and cook on LOW for 5 hours.

3. Move two shallow serving dishes or bowls next to the slow cooker. Remove cover and using pot holders or oven mitts, carefully open each liner and remove the solids with a slotted spoon or tongs to its own serving bowl. Still using a pot holder, gather the top of the first liner, carefully lift the bag from the slow cooker and move over its serving bowl. Cut a corner off the bottom of the bag, large enough to allow the remaining contents of the bag to be released into the bowl. Discard the liner. Repeat with the second liner.

4. Allow the recipe not being served to cool, and package in a resealable plastic freezer bag or freezer container. Label and freeze up to 3 months.

5. Before serving, taste, and season again with salt and pepper. Top Indian Chicken Stew with reserved pine nuts before serving.

A. CHICKEN WITH DRIED FRUIT AND MUSTARD SAUCE

SERVES 2

Fruity and peppery, this dish is a festival of color and has a celebratory taste.

2 boneless, skinless chicken breasts
Salt and freshly ground pepper, to taste
1 small onion, diced
2 cloves garlic, minced, or 1 teaspoon bottled
 minced garlic
1/2 red bell pepper, cored, seeded, and thinly
 sliced
1/4 cup chopped dried apricots
1/4 cup golden or regular raisins
2 tablespoons Dijon mustard
1/2 cup apple juice

1. Insert liner into the slow cooker, fully opening the bag and draping the excess over the sides.

2. Add chicken to the bottom of the liner. Season with salt and pepper.

3. Top with onion, garlic, and bell pepper.

4. Move the apricots and raisins to a small bowl. Stir the mustard into apple juice and pour over fruit.

5. Pour fruit mixture over the chicken and vegetables.

6. Fold the top of the bag over to one side and push ingredients at bottom of liner to over create room for the second bag.

7. Follow directions for the second recipe.

continued >

B. CHICKEN WITH PLUM SAUCE

SERVES 2

Big depth of flavor here, enhanced by the plum sauce. Slightly tangy and slightly sweet, plum sauce is made with vinegar, garlic, onions, and sweet plums.

---

2 boneless, skinless chicken breasts

Salt and freshly ground black pepper, to taste

2 cloves garlic, minced, or 1 teaspoon bottled minced garlic

1 celery rib, thinly sliced

1 tablespoon dry sherry

1 tablespoon soy sauce

1 tablespoon rice vinegar

2 tablespoons plum sauce

1 tablespoon freshly grated ginger, or 1 teaspoon ground ginger

¼ teaspoon Chinese five-spice powder

1. Insert liner into the remaining space in the slow cooker, fully opening the bag and draping the excess over the sides.

2. Add chicken to the bottom of the liner. Season with salt and pepper.

3. Add garlic and celery.

4. Stir together sherry, soy sauce, vinegar, plum sauce, ginger, and five-spice in a small bowl. Pour over chicken.

5. Fold the top of the bag over to the opposite side of the first bag and nestle the ingredients of both bags so that they are sharing the space evenly.

TO COMPLETE THE RECIPES:

1. Each closed liner should be draping away from the other, extending over the sides of the slow cooker.

2. Cover and cook on LOW for 4 hours.

3. Move two shallow serving dishes or bowls next to the slow cooker. Remove cover and using pot holders or oven mitts, carefully open each liner and remove the solids with a slotted spoon or tongs to its own serving bowl. Still using a pot holder, gather the top of the first liner, carefully lift the bag from the slow cooker and move over its serving bowl. Cut a corner off the bottom of the bag, large enough to allow the remaining contents of the bag to be released into the bowl. Discard the liner. Repeat with the second liner.

4. Allow the recipe not being served to cool, and package in a resealable plastic freezer bag or freezer container. Label and freeze up to 3 months.

5. Before serving, taste, and season again with salt and pepper.

A. CHICKEN MARSALA WITH MUSHROOMS AND SAGE

SERVES 2

Marsala is a fortified wine with a smoky, slightly sweet flavor. With the addition of mushrooms and sage, this dish has an earthy, woodsy taste.

2 boneless, skinless chicken breasts
Salt and freshly ground black pepper, to taste
4 ounces sliced mushrooms
1 small shallot, diced
2 garlic cloves, minced, or 1 teaspoon bottled minced garlic
1/3 cup chicken broth
1/3 cup Marsala wine
2 tablespoons chopped fresh parsley, divided
1 tablespoon chopped fresh sage, divided

1. Insert liner into the slow cooker, fully opening the bag and draping the excess over the sides.

2. Add chicken to the bottom of the liner. Season with salt and pepper.

3. Top chicken with mushrooms.

4. Stir together shallot, garlic, chicken broth, and wine in a small bowl. Pour over chicken.

5. Top chicken with half the parsley and half the sage, reserving the remaining parsley and sage to top finished dish for serving.

6. Fold the top of the bag over to one side and push ingredients at bottom of liner over to create room for the second bag.

7. Follow directions for the second recipe.

continued >

B. CHUNKY CHICKEN SOUP WITH GARLIC AND THYME

SERVES 2

A diagnosis of a cold isn't necessary to enjoy this chunky chicken soup. We'll add cooked egg noodles to the finished soup, but it's also very tasty without noodles.

2 boneless, skinless chicken breasts, cut into small dice
Salt, to taste
10 baby carrots, sliced
1 small onion, chopped
2 sprigs fresh thyme, or 1/2 teaspoon dried thyme
1/4 teaspoon garlic powder
1/3 cup chicken broth
Freshly ground black pepper, to taste

1. Insert liner into the remaining space in the slow cooker, fully opening the bag and draping the excess over the sides.

2. Add chicken to the bottom of the liner. Season with salt.

3. Top chicken with carrots, onions, and fresh thyme.

4. Stir together garlic powder and chicken broth in a small bowl. Pour over chicken.

5. Reserve pepper to top finished dish for serving.

6. Fold the top of the bag over to the opposite side of the first bag and nestle the ingredients of both bags so that they are sharing the space evenly.

TO COMPLETE THE RECIPES:

1. Each closed liner should be draping away from the other, extending over the sides of the slow cooker.

2. Cover and cook on LOW for 4 hours.

3. Move two shallow serving dishes or bowls next to the slow cooker. Remove cover and using pot holders or oven mitts, carefully open each liner and remove the solids with a slotted spoon or tongs to its own serving bowl. Still using a pot holder, gather the top of the first liner, carefully lift the bag from the slow cooker and move over its serving bowl. Cut a corner off the bottom of the bag, large enough to allow the

remaining contents of the bag to be released into the bowl. Discard the liner. Repeat with the second liner.

4. Allow the recipe not being served to cool, and package in a resealable plastic freezer bag or freezer container. Label and freeze up to 3 months.

5. Before serving, taste, and season as needed. Top the Chicken Marsala with Mushrooms and Sage with reserved parsley and sage before serving. Top the Chunky Chicken Soup with Garlic and Thyme with reserved pepper before serving.

A. CHICKEN PARMESAN
SERVES 2

Chicken Parmesan was one of my favorite meals to order out on those special occasions growing up when we ate at our neighborhood Italian restaurant. I've loved red-checked tablecloths ever since.

2 boneless, skinless chicken breasts
Salt and freshly ground black pepper, to taste
2 teaspoons Italian seasoning
1 (8-ounce can) tomato sauce
2 tablespoons tomato paste
½ teaspoon granulated sugar
½ teaspoon garlic powder
½ teaspoon dried basil
1 cup shredded mozzarella cheese
¼ cup shredded or grated Parmesan cheese

1. Insert liner into the slow cooker, fully opening the bag and draping the excess over the sides.

2. Add chicken to the bottom of the liner. Season with salt, pepper, and Italian seasoning.

3. Stir together tomato sauce, tomato paste, sugar, garlic powder, and basil in a medium bowl. Pour over chicken.

4. Reserve mozzarella and Parmesan cheeses to top finished dish for serving.

5. Fold the top of the bag over to one side and push ingredients at bottom of liner over to create room for the second bag.

6. Follow directions for the second recipe.

continued >

B. RASPBERRY DIJON CHICKEN
SERVES 2

Raspberry preserves create a delicious sauce for this slightly sweet, yet slightly sophisticated chicken.

---

2 boneless, skinless chicken breasts
Salt and freshly ground black pepper, to taste
1 small onion, diced
1 teaspoon Dijon mustard
1 tablespoon apple cider vinegar
1 tablespoon brown sugar
1 tablespoon Worcestershire sauce
2 tablespoons raspberry preserves
¼ cup orange juice

1. Insert liner into the remaining space in the slow cooker, fully opening the bag and draping the excess over the sides.

2. Add chicken to the bottom of the liner. Season with salt and pepper.

3. Top chicken with onion.

4. Stir together mustard, vinegar, brown sugar, Worcestershire sauce, preserves, and orange juice in a small bowl. Pour over chicken.

5. Fold the top of the bag over to the opposite side of the first bag and nestle the ingredients of both bags so that they are sharing the space evenly.

TO COMPLETE THE RECIPES:

1. Each closed liner should be draping away from the other, extending over the sides of the slow cooker.

2. Cover and cook on LOW for 4 hours.

3. Move two shallow serving dishes or bowls next to the slow cooker. Remove cover and using pot holders or oven mitts, carefully open each liner and remove the solids with a slotted spoon or tongs to its own serving bowl. Still using a pot holder, gather the top of the first liner, carefully lift the bag from the slow cooker and move over its serving bowl. Cut a corner off the bottom of the bag, large enough to allow the remaining contents of the bag to be released into the bowl. Discard the liner. Repeat with the second liner.

4. Allow the recipe not being served to cool, and package in a resealable plastic freezer bag or freezer container. Label and freeze up to 3 months.

5. Before serving, taste, and season again with salt and pepper. To serve the Chicken Parmesan, top with reserved mozzarella and Parmesan and tent with foil to melt the cheeses with the heat of the chicken.

A. ORANGE CHICKEN

SERVES 2

These chicken breasts call for a tall drink with an umbrella—à la Trader Vic's! The sweetness of the marmalade is balanced with the tang of the Dijon mustard.

2 boneless, skinless chicken breasts
1 small onion, diced
1/2 cup orange juice
1 tablespoon brown sugar
1 tablespoon apple cider vinegar
1 tablespoon orange marmalade
1 tablespoon Worcestershire sauce
1 teaspoon Dijon mustard

1. Insert liner into the slow cooker, fully opening the bag and draping the excess over the sides.

2. Add chicken to the bottom of the liner.

3. Top chicken with onion.

4. Stir together orange juice, brown sugar, vinegar, marmalade, Worcestershire sauce, and mustard in a small bowl. Pour over chicken.

5. Fold the top of the bag over to one side and push ingredients at bottom of liner over to create room for the second bag.

6. Follow directions for the second recipe.

continued >

B. GREEK ISLES CHICKEN BREASTS
SERVES 2

Traditionally made with sheep's milk, feta is a brined cheese with a slightly tangy flavor. The kalamata olives make this dish a Mediterranean favorite.

2 boneless, skinless chicken breasts
Salt and freshly ground black pepper, to taste
1 small onion, diced
2 cloves garlic, minced, or 1 teaspoon bottled minced garlic
¼ cup sun-dried tomatoes
¼ cup pitted kalamata olives
¼ cup white wine, or chicken broth
2 tablespoons lemon juice
1 tablespoon balsamic vinegar
4 springs fresh tarragon, or 2 teaspoons dried tarragon
¼ cup crumbled feta cheese

1. Insert liner into the remaining space in the slow cooker, fully opening the bag and draping the excess over the sides.

2. Add chicken to the bottom of the liner. Season with salt and pepper.

3. Top chicken with onion, garlic, tomatoes, and olives.

4. Stir together wine (or broth), lemon juice, vinegar, and tarragon in a small bowl. Pour over chicken.

5. Reserve feta cheese to top finished dish for serving.

6. Fold the top of the bag over to the opposite side of the first bag and nestle the ingredients of both bags so that they are sharing the space evenly.

TO COMPLETE THE RECIPES:

1. Each closed liner should be draping away from the other, extending over the sides of the slow cooker.

2. Cover and cook on LOW for 4 hours.

3. Move two shallow serving dishes or bowls next to the slow cooker. Remove cover and using pot holders or oven mitts, carefully open each liner and remove the solids with a slotted spoon or tongs to its own serving bowl. Still using a pot holder, gather the top of the first liner, carefully lift the bag from the slow cooker and move over its serving bowl. Cut a corner off the bottom of the bag, large enough to allow the remaining contents of the bag to be released into the bowl. Discard the liner. Repeat with the second liner.

4. Allow the recipe not being served to cool, and package in a resealable plastic freezer bag or freezer container. Label and freeze up to 3 months.

5. Before serving, taste, and season again with salt and pepper. Top Greek Isles Chicken Breasts with reserved feta cheese before serving.

A. CHICKEN, FENNEL, AND CABBAGE
SERVES 2

I adore fennel and its taste and fragrance are superb in this dish. Cut to remove the stalks from the fennel bulbs and discard stalks. Slice the bulb crosswise, discarding the tough core.

¼ small head red cabbage, sliced
1 small fennel bulb, sliced
2 boneless, skinless chicken breasts
Salt and freshly ground black pepper, to taste
10 baby carrots, sliced
1 small onion, sliced
1 teaspoon dried dill
⅓ cup chicken broth

1. Insert liner into the slow cooker, fully opening the bag and draping the excess over the sides.

2. Add cabbage and fennel to the bottom of the liner.

3. Top with chicken breasts. Season with salt and pepper.

4. Add carrots and onion, and sprinkle with dill.

5. Pour chicken broth over chicken and vegetables.

6. Fold the top of the bag over to one side and push ingredients at bottom of liner over to create room for the second bag.

7. Follow directions for the second recipe.

B. CHICKEN WITH ARTICHOKES

SERVES 2

I consider fennel seed a secret weapon. It brings a certain boldness to a dish but isn't overpowering. I even use it in meatless dishes, as it reminds most of us of the taste of ground sausage, teasing the meat lover to favor the vegetarian dish.

2 boneless, skinless chicken breasts
Juice of 1 lemon
Salt and freshly ground black pepper, to taste
1 clove garlic, minced, or $1/2$ teaspoon bottled minced garlic
2 teaspoons fennel seed
1 (13-ounce can) artichoke hearts, drained and chopped

1. Insert liner into the remaining space in the slow cooker, fully opening the bag and draping the excess over the sides.

2. Add chicken to the bottom of the liner. Pour lemon juice over chicken and season with salt and pepper.

3. Top chicken with garlic, fennel seed, and artichokes.

4. Fold the top of the bag over to the opposite side of the first bag and nestle the ingredients of both bags so that they are sharing the space evenly.

TO COMPLETE THE RECIPES:

1. Each closed liner should be draping away from the other, extending over the sides of the slow cooker.

2. Cover and cook on LOW for 4 hours.

3. Move two shallow serving dishes or bowls next to the slow cooker. Remove cover and using pot holders or oven mitts, carefully open each liner and remove the solids with a slotted spoon or tongs to its own serving bowl. Still using a pot holder, gather the top of the first liner, carefully lift the bag from the slow cooker and move over its serving bowl. Cut a corner off the bottom of the bag, large enough to allow the remaining contents of the bag to be released into the bowl. Discard the liner. Repeat with the second liner.

4. Allow the recipe not being served to cool, and package in a resealable plastic freezer bag or freezer container. Label and freeze up to 3 months.

5. Before serving, taste, and season again with salt and pepper.

A. PINEAPPLE CHICKEN

SERVES 2

There was something missing from this dish, and my assistant Elise Garner suggested the red bell pepper. That was it! Serve over yellow rice.

2 boneless, skinless chicken breasts
$1/2$ red bell pepper cored, seeded, and diced
$1/2$ cup crushed pineapple
3 tablespoons brown sugar
3 tablespoons soy sauce

1. Insert liner into the slow cooker, fully opening the bag and draping the excess over the sides.

2. Add chicken to the bottom of the liner.

3. Top the chicken with bell pepper.

4. Stir together pineapple, brown sugar, and soy sauce in a small bowl. Pour over chicken.

5. Fold the top of the bag over to one side and push ingredients at bottom of liner over to create room for the second bag.

6. Follow directions for the second recipe.

continued >

B. HOISIN CHICKEN
SERVES 2

Hoisin sauce is a kind of barbecue sauce in Chinese cooking. Thick, slightly salty, and slightly sweet, the sauce enhances these chicken breasts. Serve with rice.

2 boneless, skinless chicken breasts
3 tablespoons brown sugar
2 tablespoons ketchup
1 teaspoon freshly grated ginger
2 tablespoons hoisin sauce
1 tablespoon soy sauce
Crushed red pepper flakes, optional
Toasted sesame seeds

1. Insert liner into the remaining space in the slow cooker, fully opening the bag and draping the excess over the sides.

2. Add chicken to the bottom of the liner.

3. Stir together brown sugar, ketchup, ginger, hoisin sauce, and soy sauce in a small bowl. Pour over chicken.

4. Reserve red pepper flakes and sesame seeds to top finished dish for serving.

5. Fold the top of the bag over to the opposite side of the first bag and nestle the ingredients of both bags so that they are sharing the space evenly.

TO COMPLETE THE RECIPES:

1. Each closed liner should be draping away from the other, extending over the sides of the slow cooker.

2. Cover and cook on LOW for 4 hours.

3. Move two shallow serving dishes or bowls next to the slow cooker. Remove cover and using pot holders or oven mitts, carefully open each liner and remove the solids with a slotted spoon or tongs to its own serving bowl. Still using a pot holder, gather the top of the first liner, carefully lift the bag from the slow cooker and move over its serving bowl. Cut a corner off the bottom of the bag, large enough to allow the remaining contents of the bag to be released into the bowl. Discard the liner. Repeat with the second liner.

4. Allow the recipe not being served to cool, and package in a resealable plastic freezer bag or freezer container. Label and freeze up to 3 months.

5. Before serving, taste, and season again with salt and pepper. Top the Hoisin Chicken with reserved red pepper flakes and sesame seeds before serving.

A. TURKEY BREAST TENDERLOIN WITH CRANBERRY-ORANGE SAUCE

SERVES 2

I don't need an excuse to cook with cranberries, and whole cranberry sauce makes it easy to do so. I love the snap the cranberries give any dish and the allspice brings out their zing.

1 pound turkey breast tenderloin (usually sold in packs of two, each weighing about ³/₄ pound)

Salt and freshly ground black pepper, to taste

¹/₃ cup orange juice

³/₄ cup whole cranberry sauce

2 tablespoons light or dark brown sugar

1 tablespoon soy sauce

¹/₂ teaspoon ground allspice

1. Insert liner into the slow cooker, fully opening the bag and draping the excess over the sides.

2. Add turkey to the bottom of the liner. Season with salt and pepper.

3. Stir together orange juice, cranberry sauce, brown sugar, soy sauce, and allspice in a small bowl. Pour over turkey.

4. Fold the top of the bag over to one side and push ingredients at bottom of liner over to create room for the second bag.

5. Follow directions for the second recipe.

continued >

B. KALAMATA TURKEY TENDERLOIN WITH GREEK SEASONING

SERVES 2

Sun-dried tomatoes are available both dry and packed in oil. I use the dry more often, but if the package has been in the pantry for a time, I plump them in a bit of hot water before adding them to a recipe. If all I have on hand is the oil-packed, I drain and dry them well before using.

1 pound turkey breast tenderloin (usually sold in packs of two, each weighing about ³/₄ pound)
¹/₄ cup chicken broth
1 tablespoon fresh lemon juice, or bottled lemon juice
Salt and freshly ground black pepper, to taste
¹/₄ teaspoon dried oregano
¹/₄ teaspoon dried basil
¹/₄ teaspoon garlic powder
1 small onion, chopped
¹/₂ cup kalamata or other Greek-style olives
2 tablespoons chopped sun-dried tomatoes

1. Insert liner into the remaining space in the slow cooker, fully opening the bag and draping the excess over the sides.

2. Add turkey to the bottom of the liner.

3. Pour chicken broth and lemon juice over the turkey.

4. Season with salt, pepper, oregano, basil, and garlic powder.

5. Top with onion, olives, and tomatoes.

6. Fold the top of the bag over to the opposite side of the first bag and nestle the ingredients of both bags so that they are sharing the space evenly.

TO COMPLETE THE RECIPES:

1. Each closed liner should be draping away from the other, extending over the sides of the slow cooker.

2. Cover and cook on LOW for 6 to 7 hours.

3. Move two shallow serving dishes or bowls next to the slow cooker. Remove cover and using pot holders or oven mitts, carefully open each liner and remove the solids with a slotted spoon or tongs to its own serving bowl. Still using a pot holder, gather the top of the first liner, carefully lift the bag from the slow cooker and move over its serving bowl. Cut a corner off the bottom of the bag, large enough to allow the remaining contents of the bag to be released into the bowl. Discard the liner. Repeat with the second liner.

4. Allow the recipe not being served to cool, and package in a resealable plastic freezer bag or freezer container. Label and freeze up to 3 months.

5. Before serving, taste, and season again with salt and pepper.

BEEF

There is one cut of beef that exemplifies the qualities a slow cooker can bring out in a recipe, and that is a chuck roast. Since the smallest chuck roast I can buy is 2 pounds, I cut it in half lengthwise and use both halves as a double dinner. Flank steak, bottom round, sirloin tip, and eye of the round are terrific cuts for the slow cooker, as is ground meat for meatloaf and meatballs!

A. FLANK STEAK WITH GREEN BEANS AND PORTABELLAS

SERVES 2

Flank steak is commonly available in packages weighing just over a pound. For these two recipes, I slice the flank steak in half lengthwise. To cook or serve the steak sliced, always cut across the grain to avoid producing long stringy fibers. Serve with mixed rice.

½ **pound flank steak, sliced against the grain into ½-inch slices**

Salt and freshly ground black pepper, to taste

1 small tomato, chopped

1 large portabella mushroom cap, chopped, or 1 cup chopped baby bellas

1 cup frozen or fresh green beans, cut or whole

1 cup frozen pearl onions

½ cup red wine

1 tablespoon balsamic vinegar

1 tablespoon Dijon mustard

4 sprigs fresh rosemary, divided

1. Insert liner into the slow cooker, fully opening the bag and draping the excess over the sides.

2. Add steak to the bottom of the liner. Season with salt and pepper.

3. Top steak with tomato, mushrooms, green beans, and onions.

4. Stir together wine, vinegar, and mustard in a small bowl. Pour over steak and vegetables.

5. Top steak and vegetables with 2 sprigs of rosemary.

6. Reserve remaining rosemary to top finished dish for serving.

7. Fold the top of the bag over to one side and push ingredients at bottom of liner over to create room for the second bag.

8. Follow directions for the second recipe.

continued >

B. PEPPER STEAK
SERVES 2

Red pepper flakes give this dish its zing. The Asian flavor comes from the sesame oil, soy sauce and ginger. It's delicious!

½ **pound flank steak, sliced against the grain into ½-inch slices**
Freshly ground black pepper, to taste
1 small red onion, thinly sliced
1 red bell pepper, cored, seeded, and thinly sliced
2 cloves garlic, minced, or 1 teaspoon bottled minced garlic
¼ **cup beef broth**
1 teaspoon sesame oil
1 tablespoon dry sherry
2 tablespoons soy sauce
1 tablespoon freshly grated ginger
¼ **teaspoon crushed red pepper flakes, or more if desired**
2 tablespoons chopped fresh cilantro, or to taste

1. Insert liner into the remaining space in the slow cooker, fully opening the bag and draping the excess over the sides.

2. Add steak to the bottom of the liner. Season with pepper.

3. Top steak with onion, bell pepper, and garlic.

4. Stir together broth, sesame oil, sherry, soy sauce, and ginger in a small bowl. Pour over steak and vegetables.

5. Season with red pepper flakes.

6. Reserve cilantro to top finished dish for serving.

7. Fold the top of the bag over to the opposite side of the first bag and nestle the ingredients of both bags so that they are sharing the space evenly.

TO COMPLETE THE RECIPES:

1. Each closed liner should be draping away from the other, extending over the sides of the slow cooker.

2. Cover and cook on LOW for 5 hours.

3. Move two shallow serving dishes or bowls next to the slow cooker. Remove cover and using pot holders or oven mitts, carefully open each liner and remove the solids with a slotted spoon or tongs to its own serving bowl. Still using a pot holder, gather the top of the first liner, carefully lift the bag from the slow cooker and move over its serving bowl. Cut a corner off the bottom of the bag, large enough to allow the remaining contents of the bag to be released into the bowl. Discard the liner. Repeat with the second liner.

4. Allow the recipe not being served to cool, and package in a resealable plastic freezer bag or freezer container. Label and freeze up to 3 months.

5. Before serving, taste, and season again with salt and pepper. Top Flank Steak with Green Beans and Portabellas with reserved rosemary before serving. Top Pepper Steak with reserved cilantro before serving.

A. SOUTHWESTERN FLANK STEAK WITH A LITTLE KICK

SERVES 2

The kick comes from the chili powder, so increase the amount if you are a fan of heat. The extra squeeze of lime juice over the top of the finished dish adds a bit of pizzazz.

Half of a 1- to 1½-pound flank steak
Salt and freshly ground black pepper, to taste
½ teaspoon chili powder, or more to taste
¼ teaspoon dried oregano
1 small onion, thinly sliced
1 clove garlic, minced, or ½ teaspoon bottled minced garlic
1 green bell pepper, cored, seeded, and sliced
1½ tablespoons fresh lime juice, or bottled lime juice, divided
½ cup beef broth
1 (15-ounce) can black beans, rinsed and drained, optional

1. Insert liner into the slow cooker, fully opening the bag and draping the excess over the sides.

2. Add flank steak to the bottom of the liner. Season with salt, pepper, chili powder, and oregano.

3. Top steak with onion, garlic, and bell pepper.

4. Stir together lime juice and beef broth in a small bowl. Pour over steak and vegetables.

5. Top with black beans, if using.

6. Reserve remaining lime juice to top finished dish before serving.

7. Fold the top of the bag over to one side and push ingredients at bottom of liner over to create room for the second bag.

8. Follow directions for the second recipe.

continued >

B. FLANK STEAK FAJITAS

SERVES 2

Serve this flank steak with your favorite tortilla.

Half of a 1- to 1½-pound flank steak
Salt and freshly ground black pepper, to
    taste
1 (4-ounce) can chopped green chiles
½ small onion, sliced
½ green bell pepper, cored, seeded, and
    sliced
1 clove garlic, minced, or ½ teaspoon bottled
    minced garlic
1 (14½-ounce) can diced tomatoes
½ teaspoon chili powder
¼ teaspoon ground cumin
1 tablespoon chopped fresh parsley

1. Insert liner into the remaining space in the slow cooker, fully opening the bag and draping the excess over the sides.

2. Add flank steak to the bottom of the liner. Season with salt and pepper.

3. Top steak with green chiles, onion, bell pepper, garlic, and tomatoes.

4. Stir together chili powder, cumin and parsley in a small bowl. Sprinkle over steak and vegetables.

5. Fold the top of the bag over to the opposite side of the first bag and nestle the ingredients of both bags so that they are sharing the space evenly.

TO COMPLETE THE RECIPES:

1. Each closed liner should be draping away from the other, extending over the sides of the slow cooker.

2. Cover and cook on LOW for 6 to 7 hours.

3. Move two shallow serving dishes or bowls next to the slow cooker. Remove cover and using pot holders or oven mitts, carefully open each liner and remove the solids with a slotted spoon or tongs to its own serving bowl. Still using a pot holder, gather the top of the first liner, carefully lift the bag from the slow cooker and move over its serving bowl. Cut a corner off the bottom of the bag, large enough to allow the remaining contents of the bag to be released into the bowl. Discard the liner. Repeat with the second liner.

4. Allow the recipe not being served to cool, and package in a resealable plastic freezer bag or freezer container. Label and freeze up to 3 months.

5. Before serving, taste, and season again with salt and pepper. Top Southwestern Flank Steak with reserved lime juice.

A. MUSHROOM-STUFFED FLANK STEAK

SERVES 2

The flavor of this roll-up comes from the pesto. If you are fortunate enough to be able to grow your own basil, harvest all the last bit of basil before the end of the season and make a batch of your own. Freeze it in an ice cube tray, and transfer to a resealable plastic bag. Add it to soups and stews still frozen, or defrost to spread.

Half of a 1- to 1½-pound flank steak
2 tablespoons pesto sauce
3 tablespoons shredded or grated Parmesan cheese
6 ounces sliced fresh mushrooms
Salt and freshly ground black pepper, to taste
¼ cup beef broth

1. Insert liner into the slow cooker, fully opening the bag and draping the excess over the sides.

2. Slice flank steak open like a book. Spread evenly with pesto sauce.

3. Sprinkle with Parmesan cheese and top with mushrooms.

4. Roll up the steak from the long side and secure with wooden skewers or toothpicks.

5. Season with salt and pepper.

6. Add steak to the bottom of the liner.

7. Pour broth over steak.

8. Fold the top of the bag over to one side and push ingredients at bottom of liner over to create room for the second bag.

9. Follow directions for the second recipe.

B. RED WINE FLANK STEAK

SERVES 2

I'm not sure which I like fresh rosemary with more: chicken or beef. In any case, this is a marvelous dish, with the red wine tenderizing the beef.

Half of a 1- to 1½-pound flank steak
Salt and freshly ground black pepper, to taste
¼ teaspoon crushed red pepper flakes
2 cloves garlic, minced, or 1 teaspoon bottled minced garlic
2 tablespoons fresh lemon juice, or bottled lemon juice
¾ cup dry red wine
2 sprigs fresh rosemary, or ½ teaspoon dried rosemary, crushed

1. Insert liner into the remaining space in the slow cooker, fully opening the bag and draping the excess over the sides.

2. Add flank steak to the bottom of the liner. Season with salt and pepper.

3. Stir together red pepper flakes, garlic, lemon juice, and red wine in a small bowl. Pour over steak.

4. Top steak with rosemary.

5. Fold the top of the bag over to the opposite side of the first bag and nestle the ingredients of both bags so that they are sharing the space evenly.

TO COMPLETE THE RECIPES:

1. Each closed liner should be draping away from the other, extending over the sides of the slow cooker.

2. Cover and cook on LOW for 6 to 7 hours.

3. Move two shallow serving dishes or bowls next to the slow cooker. Remove cover and using pot holders or oven mitts, carefully open each liner and remove the solids with a slotted spoon or tongs to its own serving bowl. Still using a pot holder, gather the top of the first liner, carefully lift the bag from the slow cooker and move over its serving bowl. Cut a corner off the bottom of the bag, large enough to allow the remaining contents of the bag to be released into the bowl. Discard the liner. Repeat with the second liner.

4. Allow the recipe not being served to cool, and package in a resealable plastic freezer bag or freezer container. Label and freeze up to 3 months.

5. Before serving, taste, and season again with salt and pepper. For the Mushroom-Stuffed Flank Steak, remove the skewer and slice meat before serving.

A. ROSEMARY WINE POT ROAST

SERVES 2

Tried and true, pot roast calls out for red wine and rosemary for classic, rustic flavor. Pearl onions are "sweet onions," small orbs of mild onion flavor. I keep them as a freezer staple so they're always on hand—and no chopping is a bonus for quick prep.

1 pound chuck roast (from cutting a 2-pound chuck roast in half lengthwise)
Salt and freshly ground black pepper, to taste
10 baby carrots, sliced
1 cup frozen pearl onions
2 cloves garlic, minced, or 1 teaspoon bottled minced garlic
1/2 cup beef broth
1/2 cup red wine
2 tablespoons tomato paste
2 sprigs fresh rosemary

1. Insert liner into the slow cooker, fully opening the bag and draping the excess over the sides.

2. Add roast to the bottom of the liner. Season with salt and pepper.

3. Top roast with carrots, onions, and garlic.

4. Stir together broth, wine, and tomato paste in a small bowl. Pour over roast and vegetables.

5. Top roast and vegetables with rosemary.

6. Fold the top of the bag over to one side and push ingredients at bottom of liner over to create room for the second bag.

7. Follow directions for the second recipe.

continued >

B. BEEF STEW WITH BUTTERNUT SQUASH
SERVES 2

Nutmeg and allspice usher in the autumn flavors. The butternut squash can be difficult to cut. I recommend cutting it in half lengthwise, then peeling with a potato peeler. Scrape out seeds and cut flesh into small dice before adding to the crock.

1 pound chuck roast (from cutting a 2-pound chuck roast in half lengthwise), cut into 1-inch chunks
Salt and freshly ground black pepper, to taste
1 cup diced butternut squash
1 small onion, chopped
½ cup beef broth
1 (8-ounce) can tomato sauce
1 tablespoon Worcestershire sauce
⅛ teaspoon ground nutmeg
⅛ teaspoon ground allspice
2 cloves garlic, minced, or 1 teaspoon bottled minced garlic

1. Insert liner into the remaining space in the slow cooker, fully opening the bag and draping the excess over the sides.

2. Add chuck roast to the bottom of the liner. Season with salt and pepper.

3. Top roast with squash and onion.

4. Stir together broth, tomato sauce, Worcestershire sauce, nutmeg, allspice, and garlic in a small bowl. Pour over beef and vegetables.

5. Fold the top of the bag over to the opposite side of the first bag and nestle the ingredients of both bags so that they are sharing the space evenly.

TO COMPLETE THE RECIPES:

1. Each closed liner should be draping away from the other, extending over the sides of the slow cooker.

2. Cover and cook on LOW for 7 hours.

3. Move two shallow serving dishes or bowls next to the slow cooker. Remove cover and using pot holders or oven mitts, carefully open each liner and remove the solids with a slotted spoon or tongs to its own serving bowl. Still using a pot holder, gather the top of the first liner, carefully lift the bag from the slow cooker and move over its serving bowl. Cut a corner off the bottom of the bag, large enough to allow the remaining contents of the bag to be released into the bowl. Discard the liner. Repeat with the second liner.

4. Allow the recipe not being served to cool, and package in a resealable plastic freezer bag or freezer container. Label and freeze up to 3 months.

5. Before serving, taste, and season again with salt and pepper.

A. PEPPERY BOTTOM ROUND

SERVES 2

Be generous with your pepper grinding here. It's the base of this delicious dish, complemented by Worcestershire sauce.

Half of a 2-pound bottom round roast
Salt and freshly ground black pepper, to taste
1 small carrot, chopped
1 small onion, chopped
1 rib celery, chopped
2 tablespoons Worcestershire sauce
1/2 teaspoon garlic powder
2 springs fresh thyme, or 1/2 teaspoon dried thyme

1. Insert liner into the slow cooker, fully opening the bag and draping the excess over the sides.

2. Add roast to the bottom of the liner. Season with salt and pepper.

3. Top roast with carrot, onion, and celery.

4. Stir together Worcestershire sauce and garlic powder in a small bowl. Pour over beef and vegetables.

5. Place thyme on top of roast and vegetables.

6. Fold the top of the bag over to one side and push ingredients at bottom of liner over to create room for the second bag.

7. Follow directions for the second recipe.

continued >

B. FALL-FLAVORED BOTTOM ROUND
SERVES 2

Port wine is a fortified wine from Portugal and gives this dish, along with the dried fruit, its sweet taste. Mashed sweet potatoes make a fine side dish.

Half of a 2-pound bottom round roast
Salt and freshly ground black pepper, to taste
½ cup mixed dried fruit, chopped, such as apricots, cranberries, and raisins
1 small onion, chopped
½ cup port wine

1. Insert liner into the remaining space in the slow cooker, fully opening the bag and draping the excess over the sides.

2. Add roast to the bottom of the liner. Season with salt and pepper.

3. Top roast with mixed dried fruit and onion.

4. Pour wine over roast.

5. Fold the top of the bag over to the opposite side of the first bag and nestle the ingredients of both bags so that they are sharing the space evenly.

TO COMPLETE THE RECIPES:

1. Each closed liner should be draping away from the other, extending over the sides of the slow cooker.

2. Cover and cook on LOW for 6 hours.

3. Move two shallow serving dishes or bowls next to the slow cooker. Remove cover and using pot holders or oven mitts, carefully open each liner and remove the solids with a slotted spoon or tongs to its own serving bowl. Still using a pot holder, gather the top of the first liner, carefully lift the bag from the slow cooker and move over its serving bowl. Cut a corner off the bottom of the bag, large enough to allow the remaining contents of the bag to be released into the bowl. Discard the liner. Repeat with the second liner.

4. Allow the recipe not being served to cool, and package in a resealable plastic freezer bag or freezer container. Label and freeze up to 3 months.

5. Before serving, taste, and season again with salt and pepper.

A. POT ROAST WITH VEGETABLES AND FETA

SERVES 2

Slightly sweet and slightly tart, this pot roast is a hearty dish. The orange zest, feta cheese, and pine nuts provide a fresh, crunchy finish.

1 pound chuck roast (from cutting a 2-pound chuck roast in half lengthwise)

Salt and freshly ground black pepper, to taste

1 bay leaf

1 small onion, thinly sliced

2 cloves garlic, minced, or 1 teaspoon bottled minced garlic

1 small eggplant, peeled and cut into 1/2-inch cubes

1/2 red bell pepper, cored, seeded, and sliced

1/2 cup red wine

1/2 cup beef broth

2 tablespoons tomato paste

2 tablespoons light or dark brown sugar

1 tablespoon balsamic vinegar

1 teaspoon dried oregano

1/2 teaspoon ground cloves

2 tablespoons grated orange zest, no white attached, divided

1/4 cup crumbled feta cheese

1/4 cup pine nuts

1. Insert liner into the slow cooker, fully opening the bag and draping the excess over the sides.

2. Add pot roast to bottom of liner. Season with salt and pepper.

3. Top roast with bay leaf, onion, garlic, eggplant, and bell pepper.

4. Stir together wine, broth, tomato paste, brown sugar, vinegar, oregano, and cloves in a small bowl. Pour over roast and vegetables.

5. Sprinkle roast and vegetables with 1 tablespoon orange zest.

6. Reserve remaining zest, feta cheese, and pine nuts to top finished dish for serving.

7. Fold the top of the bag over to one side and push ingredients at bottom of liner over to create room for the second bag.

8. Follow directions for the second recipe.

continued >

B. OLD-FASHIONED POT ROAST
SERVES 2

Potatoes are slow cooker favorites, but because of their density, care should be taken with their size. Here I call for half-inch or smaller cubes.

1 pound chuck roast (from cutting a 2-pound chuck roast in half lengthwise)
Salt and freshly ground black pepper, to taste
1 bay leaf
2 small white potatoes, peeled and cut into ½-inch cubes
½ cup frozen or fresh green beans, cut or whole
10 baby carrots, sliced
1 cup frozen pearl onions
1 cup beef broth
1 tablespoon tomato paste
2 teaspoons Worcestershire sauce
2 sprigs fresh oregano, or 1 teaspoon dried oregano

1. Insert liner into the remaining space in the slow cooker, fully opening the bag and draping the excess over the sides.

2. Add chuck roast to bottom of liner. Season with salt and pepper.

3. Top with bay leaf, potatoes, green beans, carrots, and onions.

4. Stir together beef broth, tomato paste, Worcestershire sauce, and oregano in a small bowl. Pour over roast and vegetables.

5. Fold the top of the bag over to the opposite side of the first bag and nestle the ingredients of both bags so that they are sharing the space evenly.

TO COMPLETE THE RECIPES:

1. Each closed liner should be draping away from the other, extending over the sides of the slow cooker.

2. Cover and cook on LOW for 7 hours.

3. Move two shallow serving dishes or bowls next to the slow cooker. Remove cover and using pot holders or oven mitts, carefully open each liner and remove the solids with a slotted spoon or tongs to its own serving bowl. Still using a pot holder, gather the top of the first liner, carefully lift the bag from the slow cooker and move over its serving bowl. Cut a corner off the bottom of the bag, large enough to allow the remaining contents of the bag to be released into the bowl. Discard the liner. Repeat with the second liner.

4. Allow the recipe not being served to cool, and package in a resealable plastic freezer bag or freezer container. Label and freeze up to 3 months.

5. Before serving, taste, and season again with salt and pepper. Remove bay leaves and top Pot Roast with Vegetables and Feta with reserved orange zest, feta cheese and pine nuts before serving.

A. INDIA-INSPIRED POT ROAST
SERVES 2

Very tender and juicy, this pot roast makes me think of a trip on the Orient Express.

1 pound chuck roast (from cutting a 2-pound chuck roast in half lengthwise)
Salt and freshly ground black pepper, to taste
1 parsnip, peeled and diced
10 baby carrots, chopped
1 white potato, diced
1 small onion, diced
1/2 cup beef broth
2 teaspoons garam masala
1 teaspoon turmeric powder
1/2 teaspoon chili powder
2 cloves garlic, minced, or 1 teaspoon bottled minced garlic
1/2 teaspoon freshly grated ginger

1. Insert liner into the slow cooker, fully opening the bag and draping the excess over the sides.

2. Add chuck roast to the bottom of the liner. Season with salt and pepper.

3. Top roast with parsnip, carrots, potato, and onion.

4. Stir together broth, garam masala, turmeric, chili powder, garlic, and ginger in a small bowl. Pour over beef and vegetables.

5. Fold the top of the bag over to one side and push ingredients at bottom of liner over to create room for the second bag.

6. Follow directions for the second recipe.

B. DILLED POT ROAST

SERVES 2

I loved that one of my testers described this dish as "elegant, Christmas-y."

1 pound chuck roast (from cutting a 2-pound chuck roast in half lengthwise)
Salt and freshly ground black pepper, to taste
1 cup frozen pearl onions
10 baby carrots, chopped
4 ounces fresh sliced mushrooms
1 bay leaf
1/2 cup red wine
1/2 cup beef broth
1 teaspoon dried dill weed
1 tablespoon chopped fresh parsley

1. Insert liner into the remaining space in the slow cooker, fully opening the bag and draping the excess over the sides.

2. Add chuck roast to the bottom of the liner. Season with salt and pepper.

3. Top roast with onions, carrots, mushrooms, and bay leaf.

4. Stir together wine, broth and dill weed in a small bowl. Pour over roast and vegetables.

5. Reserve parsley to top finished dish for serving.

6. Fold the top of the bag over to the opposite side of the first bag and nestle the ingredients of both bags so that they are sharing the space evenly.

TO COMPLETE THE RECIPES:

1. Each closed liner should be draping away from the other, extending over the sides of the slow cooker.

2. Cover and cook on LOW for 7 hours.

3. Move 2 shallow serving dishes or bowls next to the slow cooker. Remove cover and using pot holders or oven mitts, carefully open each liner and remove the solids with a slotted spoon or tongs to its own serving bowl. Still using a pot holder, gather the top of the first liner, carefully lift the bag from the slow cooker and move over its serving bowl. Cut a corner off the bottom of the bag, large enough to allow the remaining contents of the bag to be released into the bowl. Discard the liner. Repeat with the second liner.

4. Allow the recipe not being served to cool, and package in a resealable plastic freezer bag or freezer container. Label and freeze up to 3 months.

5. Before serving, taste, and season again with salt and pepper. Remove bay leaf and top the Dilled Pot Roast with reserved parsley before serving.

A. LIME-LEMON POT ROAST WITH TOMATO SAUCE
SERVES 2

I owe Nathalie Dupree a debt of gratitude for this recipe, now a classic, from her book *New Southern Cooking*. It's simply the best dish to ever come out of a slow cooker.

1 pound chuck roast (from cutting a 2-pound chuck roast in half lengthwise)

Salt and freshly ground black pepper, to taste

Grated zest of 1 lime, no white attached, divided

Grated zest of 1 lemon, no white attached, divided

3 tablespoons fresh lime juice, or bottled lime juice

2 cloves garlic, minced, or 1 teaspoon bottled minced garlic

1 cup beef broth

½ teaspoon dried Italian seasoning

1 (14-ounce) can crushed tomatoes

1. Insert liner into the slow cooker, fully opening the bag and draping the excess over the sides.

2. Add roast to the bottom of the liner. Season with salt and pepper.

3. Sprinkle half of the lime and lemon zests on roast.

4. Reserve remaining zests to top finished dish for serving.

5. Stir together lime juice, garlic, beef broth, Italian seasoning, and crushed tomatoes in a medium bowl. Pour over roast.

6. Fold the top of the bag over to one side and push ingredients at bottom of liner over to create room for the second bag.

7. Follow directions for the second recipe.

continued >

B. VINEGAR-BRAISED POT ROAST

SERVES 2

Coffee adds a deep flavor to braised meats. I keep a few packets of instant coffee from that addictive national-chain coffee house on hand for just such recipes.

1 pound chuck roast (from cutting a 2-pound chuck roast in half lengthwise)

Salt and freshly ground black pepper, to taste

1 small onion, sliced

$\frac{1}{2}$ cup strong coffee

1 tablespoon balsamic vinegar

2 sprigs rosemary, or $\frac{1}{2}$ teaspoon dried rosemary, crushed

1. Insert liner into the remaining space in the slow cooker, fully opening the bag and draping the excess over the sides.

2. Add roast to the bottom of the liner. Season with salt and pepper.

3. Top roast with onion.

4. Stir together coffee and balsamic vinegar in a small bowl. Pour over roast and onion.

5. Place rosemary on top of roast.

6. Fold the top of the bag over to the opposite side of the first bag and nestle the ingredients of both bags so that they are sharing the space evenly.

TO COMPLETE THE RECIPES:

1. Each closed liner should be draping away from the other, extending over the sides of the slow cooker.

2. Cover and cook on LOW for 8 hours.

3. Move two shallow serving dishes or bowls next to the slow cooker. Remove cover and using pot holders or oven mitts, carefully open each liner and remove the solids with a slotted spoon or tongs to its own serving bowl. Still using a pot holder, gather the top of the first liner, carefully lift the bag from the slow cooker and move over its serving bowl. Cut a corner off the bottom of the bag, large enough to allow the remaining contents of the bag to be released into the bowl. Discard the liner. Repeat with the second liner.

4. Allow the recipe not being served to cool, and package in a resealable plastic freezer bag or freezer container. Label and freeze up to 3 months.

5. Before serving, taste, and season again with salt and pepper. Top Lime-Lemon Pot Roast with Tomato Sauce with reserved zests.

A. SWEET TOMATO POT ROAST
SERVES 2

Holiday flavors come to mind with this roast. The splash of vinegar is tempered by the ginger and cinnamon.

1 pound chuck roast (from cutting a 2-pound chuck roast in half lengthwise)
Salt and freshly ground black pepper, to taste
$1/2$ cup cranberry juice
1 (8-ounce) can tomato sauce
1 tablespoon white or cider vinegar
1 small onion, chopped
1 teaspoon freshly grated ginger, or $1/2$ teaspoon ground ginger
1 teaspoon ground cinnamon

1. Insert liner into the slow cooker, fully opening the bag and draping the excess over the sides.

2. Add roast to the bottom of the liner. Season with salt and pepper.

3. Stir together cranberry juice, tomato sauce, vinegar, onion, ginger, and cinnamon in a small bowl. Pour over roast.

4. Fold the top of the bag over to one side and push ingredients at bottom of liner over to create room for the second bag.

5. Follow directions for the second recipe.

B. HORSERADISH POT ROAST WITH VEGETABLES
SERVES 2

I grew horseradish in my first herb garden and have grown it ever since. Its naturally sharp flavor becomes milder during cooking.

1 pound chuck roast (from cutting a 2-pound chuck roast in half lengthwise)
Salt and freshly ground black pepper, to taste
1 small baking potato, peeled and cut into ¹/₂-inch chunks
1 medium carrot, cut into ¹/₂-inch chunks
1 small onion, chopped
1 cup beef broth
¹/₄ cup red wine
1 tablespoon vinegar
1 tablespoon ketchup
1 tablespoon prepared horseradish
1 tablespoon Dijon mustard
1 teaspoon granulated sugar

1. Insert liner into the remaining space in the slow cooker, fully opening the bag and draping the excess over the sides.

2. Add roast to the bottom of the liner. Season with salt and pepper.

3. Top roast with potato, carrot and onion.

4. Stir together broth, wine, vinegar, ketchup, horseradish, mustard, and sugar in a small bowl. Pour over roast and vegetables.

5. Fold the top of the bag over to the opposite side of the first bag and nestle the ingredients of both bags so that they are sharing the space evenly.

TO COMPLETE THE RECIPES:

1. Each closed liner should be draping away from the other, extending over the sides of the slow cooker.

2. Cover and cook on LOW for 8 hours.

3. Move two shallow serving dishes or bowls next to the slow cooker. Remove cover and using pot holders or oven mitts, carefully open each liner and remove the solids with a slotted spoon or tongs to its own serving bowl. Still using a pot holder, gather the top of the first liner, carefully lift the bag from the slow cooker and move over its serving bowl. Cut a corner off the bottom of the bag, large enough to allow the remaining contents of the bag to be released into the bowl. Discard the liner. Repeat with the second liner.

4. Allow the recipe not being served to cool, and package in a resealable plastic freezer bag or freezer container. Label and freeze up to 3 months.

5. Before serving, taste, and season again with salt and pepper.

A. HOISIN SHORT RIBS

SERVES 2

Beef short ribs are full of flavor and become melt-in-your-mouth tender in the slow cooker.

2 pounds beef short ribs
Freshly ground black pepper, to taste
10 baby carrots, chopped
1 small white potato, diced
$1/2$ cup hoisin sauce

1. Insert liner into the slow cooker, fully opening the bag and draping the excess over the sides.

2. Add short ribs to the bottom of the liner. Season with pepper.

3. Top short ribs with carrots and potato.

4. Stir in the hoisin sauce to coat ribs and vegetables.

5. Fold the top of the bag over to one side and push ingredients at bottom of liner over to create room for the second bag.

6. Follow directions for the second recipe.

B. BRAISED SHORT RIBS
SERVES 2

We like the touch of sweetness from the brown sugar in these short ribs.

2 pounds beef short ribs
Salt and freshly ground black pepper, to taste
1 small onion, diced
1 (8-ounce) can tomato sauce
¼ cup red wine
1 teaspoon Worcestershire sauce
1 tablespoon brown sugar
1 clove garlic, minced, or ½ teaspoon bottled minced garlic

1. Insert liner into the remaining space in the slow cooker, fully opening the bag and draping the excess over the sides.

2. Add short ribs to the bottom of the liner. Season with salt and pepper.

3. Top short ribs with onion.

4. Stir together tomato sauce, wine, Worcestershire sauce, brown sugar, and garlic in a small bowl. Pour over short ribs.

5. Fold the top of the bag over to the opposite side of the first bag and nestle the ingredients of both bags so that they are sharing the space evenly.

TO COMPLETE THE RECIPES:

1. Each closed liner should be draping away from the other, extending over the sides of the slow cooker.

2. Cover and cook on HIGH for 4 hours.

3. Move two shallow serving dishes or bowls next to the slow cooker. Remove cover and using pot holders or oven mitts, carefully open each liner and remove the solids with a slotted spoon or tongs to its own serving bowl. Still using a pot holder, gather the top of the first liner, carefully lift the bag from the slow cooker and move over its serving bowl. Cut a corner off the bottom of the bag, large enough to allow the remaining contents of the bag to be released into the bowl. Discard the liner. Repeat with the second liner.

4. Allow the recipe not being served to cool, and package in a resealable plastic freezer bag or freezer container. Label and freeze up to 3 months.

5. Before serving, taste, and season again with salt and pepper.

A. EYE OF ROUND IN MARSALA

SERVES 2

The eye of the round is the leanest cut of beef. Lean means low fat and often translates to low flavor. Not here, though, cooking low and slow with broth and Marsala wine.

---

4 ounces sliced mushrooms

1 small onion, sliced

2 cloves garlic, minced, or 1 teaspoon bottled minced garlic

10 baby carrots, sliced

Half of a 2-pound eye of round roast

Salt and freshly ground black pepper, to taste

1/2 cup beef broth

1/2 cup Marsala wine

2 teaspoons dried oregano

1. Insert liner into the slow cooker, fully opening the bag and draping the excess over the sides.

2. Add mushrooms, onion, garlic, and carrots to the bottom of the liner.

3. Top vegetables with roast. Season with salt and pepper.

4. Stir together beef broth, Marsala, and oregano in a small bowl. Pour over roast and vegetables.

5. Fold the top of the bag over to one side and push ingredients at bottom of liner over to create room for the second bag.

6. Follow directions for the second recipe.

continued >

B. EYE OF ROUND IN MUSTARD SAUCE

SERVES 2

Spicy brown mustard is a pantry staple for me.

Half of a 2-pound eye of round roast
Salt and freshly ground black pepper, to
   taste
1 small onion, sliced
1/2 cup beef broth
2 tablespoons spicy brown mustard
1 teaspoon garlic powder

1. Insert liner into the remaining space in the slow cooker, fully opening the bag and draping the excess over the sides.

2. Add roast to the bottom of liner. Season with salt and pepper.

3. Top roast with onion.

4. Stir together beef broth, mustard, and garlic powder in a small bowl. Pour over roast.

5. Fold the top of the bag over to the opposite side of the first bag and nestle the ingredients of both bags so that they are sharing the space evenly.

TO COMPLETE THE RECIPES:

1. Each closed liner should be draping away from the other, extending over the sides of the slow cooker.

2. Cover and cook on LOW for 6 hours.

3. Move two shallow serving dishes or bowls next to the slow cooker. Remove cover and using pot holders or oven mitts, carefully open each liner and remove the solids with a slotted spoon or tongs to its own serving bowl. Still using a pot holder, gather the top of the first liner, carefully lift the bag from the slow cooker and move over its serving bowl. Cut a corner off the bottom of the bag, large enough to allow the remaining contents of the bag to be released into the bowl. Discard the liner. Repeat with the second liner.

4. Allow the recipe not being served to cool, and package in a resealable plastic freezer bag or freezer container. Label and freeze up to 3 months.

5. Before serving, taste, and season again with salt and pepper.

A. MEATLOAF

SERVES 2

Meatloaf appeared in regular rotation in our house as I was growing up. I only wish Mom had known about fresh basil.

2 tablespoons milk
¼ cup seasoned breadcrumbs
1 large egg yolk
1 tablespoon Dijon mustard
1 tablespoon Worcestershire sauce
1 small onion, finely chopped
1 clove garlic, minced, or ½ teaspoon bottled minced garlic
¼ cup chopped fresh basil, divided
½ pound lean ground beef
1 (8-ounce) can tomato sauce

1. Insert liner into the slow cooker, fully opening the bag and draping the excess over the sides.

2. Stir together milk, breadcrumbs, egg yolk, mustard, Worcestershire sauce, onion, garlic, and 3 tablespoons basil in a medium bowl.

3. Add ground beef and use hands to mix until well combined.

4. Form meat mixture into a loaf and add to the bottom of the liner. Pour tomato sauce over meatloaf.

5. Reserve remaining basil to top finished dish before serving.

6. Fold the top of the bag over to one side and push ingredients at bottom of liner over to create room for the second bag.

7. Follow directions for the second recipe.

continued >

B. MEATBALLS
SERVES 2

These meatballs cook in their own sauce, producing moist, tender spheres of homemade goodness.

¼ cup seasoned breadcrumbs
⅓ cup milk
½ small onion, finely chopped
Salt and freshly ground black pepper, to taste
½ pound lean ground beef
⅓ cup ketchup
2 tablespoons water
1 tablespoon white vinegar
1 teaspoon granulated sugar

1. Insert liner into the remaining space in the slow cooker, fully opening the bag and draping the excess over the sides.

2. Stir together breadcrumbs and milk in a small bowl. Add onion, salt, pepper, and ground beef. Use hands to mix until well combined.

3. Form into 1-inch balls (about 10) and add to the bottom of the liner.

4. Stir together ketchup, water, vinegar, and sugar in a small bowl. Pour over meatballs.

5. Fold the top of the bag over to the opposite side of the first bag and nestle the ingredients of both bags so that they are sharing the space evenly.

TO COMPLETE THE RECIPES:

1. Each closed liner should be draping away from the other, extending over the sides of the slow cooker.

2. Cover and cook on LOW for 5 hours.

3. Move two shallow serving dishes or bowls next to the slow cooker. Remove cover and using pot holders or oven mitts, carefully open each liner and remove the solids with a slotted spoon or tongs to its own serving bowl. Still using a pot holder, gather the top of the first liner, carefully lift the bag from the slow cooker and move over its serving bowl. Cut a corner off the bottom of the bag, large enough to allow the remaining contents of the bag to be released into the bowl. Discard the liner. Repeat with the second liner.

4. Allow the recipe not being served to cool, and package in a resealable plastic freezer bag or freezer container. Label and freeze up to 3 months.

5. Before serving, taste, and season again with salt and pepper. Top the Meatloaf with remaining basil before serving.

A. CHUTNEY BEEF STEW

SERVES 2

Chutney is a sweet and spicy jam-like condiment traditional in South Indian cuisine. The most widely available mango chutney is called Major Grey's, available under several brands. Major Grey, likely a fictional character, is said to have created the original recipe in Colonial India. If you find mango chutney made by a small purveyor, you'll be in for a special treat.

1/2 **pound beef stew meat**

Salt and freshly ground black pepper, to taste

1 small onion, chopped

1 cup broccoli florets

1/2 **cup beef broth**

1/4 **cup mango chutney**

2 cloves garlic, minced or 1 teaspoon bottled minced garlic

1 1/2 **teaspoons curry powder**

Crushed red pepper flakes, optional

1. Insert liner into the slow cooker, fully opening the bag and draping the excess over the sides.

2. Add beef to the bottom of the liner. Season with salt and pepper.

3. Top beef with onion and broccoli.

4. Stir together broth, chutney, garlic, and curry powder in a small bowl. Pour over beef and vegetables.

5. Reserve crushed red pepper flakes to top finished dish for serving, if desired.

6. Fold the top of the bag over to one side and push ingredients at bottom of liner over to create room for the second bag.

7. Follow directions for the second recipe.

continued >

B. BEEF AND VEGETABLE STEW WITH GINGER

SERVES 2

Fresh ginger dehydrates quickly, so I store mine in a Mason jar filled with dry sherry. It keeps for months in the refrigerator. A microplane grater makes quick work of grating the root as needed.

½ **pound beef stew meat**
Salt and freshly ground black pepper, to taste
10 baby carrots, chopped
½ **red bell pepper, cored, seeded, and sliced**
1 small leek, white part only, cleaned and thinly sliced
1 tablespoon soy sauce
2 cloves garlic, minced, or 1 teaspoon bottled minced garlic
1 tablespoon freshly grated ginger, or 1 teaspoon ground ginger
¼ **teaspoon cayenne pepper**
2 green onions, sliced, white and green parts

1. Insert liner into the remaining space in the slow cooker, fully opening the bag and draping the excess over the sides.

2. Add beef to the bottom of the liner. Season with salt and pepper.

3. Top beef with carrots, bell pepper, and leek.

4. Stir together soy sauce, garlic, ginger, and cayenne pepper in a small bowl. Pour over stew meat and stir to coat meat with mixture.

5. Reserve green onions to top finished dish before serving.

6. Fold the top of the bag over to the opposite side of the first bag and nestle the ingredients of both bags so that they are sharing the space evenly.

TO COMPLETE THE RECIPES:

1. Each closed liner should be draping away from the other, extending over the sides of the slow cooker.

2. Cover and cook on HIGH for 5 hours.

3. Move two shallow serving dishes or bowls next to the slow cooker. Remove cover and using pot holders or oven mitts, carefully open each liner and remove the solids with a slotted spoon or tongs to its own serving bowl. Still using a pot holder, gather the top of the first liner, carefully lift the bag from the slow cooker and move over its serving bowl. Cut a corner off the bottom of the bag, large enough to allow the remaining contents of the bag to be released into the bowl. Discard the liner. Repeat with the second liner.

4. Allow the recipe not being served to cool, and package in a resealable plastic freezer bag or freezer container. Label and freeze up to 3 months.

5. Before serving, taste, and season again with salt and pepper. Top Chutney Beef Stew with crushed red pepper flakes, if desired, before serving. Top the Beef and Vegetable Stew with Ginger with reserved green onions before serving.

A. SPICY MUSTARD BEEF STEW

SERVES 2

Spicy brown mustard brings an even deeper flavor to this beef stew.

½ **pound beef stew meat**
Salt and freshly ground black pepper, to
   taste
10 baby carrots, chopped
4 ounces fresh sliced mushrooms
1 small white potato, diced
½ **cup beef broth**
1 tablespoon tomato paste
2 tablespoons spicy brown mustard

1. Insert liner into the slow cooker, fully opening the bag and draping the excess over the sides.

2. Add beef to the bottom of the liner. Season with salt and pepper.

3. Top with carrots, mushrooms and potato.

4. Stir together broth, tomato paste, and mustard in a small bowl. Pour over beef and vegetables.

5. Fold the top of the bag over to one side and push ingredients at bottom of liner over to create room for the second bag.

6. Follow directions for the second recipe.

continued >

B. ASIAN BEEF STEW

SERVES 2

Not only is this a scrumptious dish, but the brown beef, orange carrots, and green asparagus make it colorfully enticing as well.

½ **pound beef stew meat**
Salt and freshly ground black pepper, to taste
¼ **pound asparagus, cut into 1-inch slices**
10 baby carrots, chopped
¼ **cup dry sherry**
2 tablespoons soy sauce
1 teaspoon dark sesame oil
1 tablespoon freshly grated ginger
2 cloves garlic, minced, or 1 teaspoon bottled minced garlic
1 teaspoon Chinese five-spice powder

1. Insert liner into the remaining space in the slow cooker, fully opening the bag and draping the excess over the sides.

2. Add beef to the bottom of the liner. Season with salt and pepper.

3. Top beef with asparagus and carrots.

4. Stir together sherry, soy sauce, sesame oil, ginger, garlic, and five-spice powder in a small bowl. Pour over beef and vegetables.

5. Fold the top of the bag over to the opposite side of the first bag and nestle the ingredients of both bags so that they are sharing the space evenly.

TO COMPLETE THE RECIPES:

1. Each closed liner should be draping away from the other, extending over the sides of the slow cooker.

2. Cover and cook on HIGH for 5 hours.

3. Move two shallow serving dishes or bowls next to the slow cooker. Remove cover and using pot holders or oven mitts, carefully open each liner and remove the solids with a slotted spoon or tongs to its own serving bowl. Still using a pot holder, gather the top of the first liner, carefully lift the bag from the slow cooker and move over its serving bowl. Cut a corner off the bottom of the bag, large enough to allow the remaining contents of the bag to be released into the bowl. Discard the liner. Repeat with the second liner.

4. Allow the recipe not being served to cool, and package in a resealable plastic freezer bag or freezer container. Label and freeze up to 3 months.

5. Before serving, taste, and season again with salt and pepper.

A. TOMATO-BASED BEEF STEW
SERVES 2

This rich and yummy stew gets a bump in nutrition from the unusual addition of spinach. If preferred, the spinach can be stirred into the hot stew just before serving, yielding wilted spinach leaves.

½ pound beef stew meat

Salt and freshly ground black pepper, to taste

1 cup frozen pearl onions

4 ounces sliced, fresh mushrooms

1 (5-ounce) package fresh baby spinach

½ cup beef broth

2 tablespoons tomato paste

1 (8-ounce) can tomato sauce

2 cloves garlic, minced, or 1 teaspoon bottled minced garlic

2 teaspoons dried oregano

1. Insert liner into the slow cooker, fully opening the bag and draping the excess over the sides.

2. Add stew meat to the bottom of the liner. Season with salt and pepper.

3. Top meat with onions, mushrooms, and spinach.

4. Stir together broth, tomato paste, tomato sauce, garlic, and oregano in a small bowl. Pour over meat and vegetables.

5. Fold the top of the bag over to one side and push ingredients at bottom of liner over to create room for the second bag.

6. Follow directions for the second recipe.

B. MUSHROOM BEEF STEW
SERVES 2

Nearly twenty years ago, my dear friend Miegan Gordon presented me with a bay plant to add to my herb garden. Today it is a twelve-foot-tall bay tree! If fresh bay leaves are available, they may be substituted in the same quantity as the dried. Always remove bay leaves before serving the finished dish.

½ pound beef stew meat

Salt and freshly ground black pepper, to taste

½ teaspoon paprika

¼ teaspoon ground cinnamon

4 ounces sliced fresh mushrooms

1 small tomato, diced

1 small onion, diced

1 bay leaf

¼ cup white wine

¼ cup beef broth

1. Insert liner into the remaining space in the slow cooker, fully opening the bag and draping the excess over the sides.

2. Add stew meat to the bottom of the liner. Season with salt, pepper, paprika, and cinnamon.

3. Top meat with mushrooms, tomato, onion, and bay leaf.

4. Stir together wine and broth in a small bowl. Pour over meat and vegetables.

5. Fold the top of the bag over to the opposite side of the first bag and nestle the ingredients of both bags so that they are sharing the space evenly.

TO COMPLETE THE RECIPES:

1. Each closed liner should be draping away from the other, extending over the sides of the slow cooker.

2. Cover and cook on LOW for 7 hours.

3. Move two shallow serving dishes or bowls next to the slow cooker. Remove cover and using pot holders or oven mitts, carefully open each liner and remove the solids with a slotted spoon or tongs to its own serving bowl. Still using a pot holder, gather the top of the first liner, carefully lift the bag from the slow cooker and move over its serving bowl. Cut a corner off the bottom of the bag, large enough to allow the remaining contents of the bag to be released into the bowl. Discard the liner. Repeat with the second liner.

4. Allow the recipe not being served to cool, and package in a resealable plastic freezer bag or freezer container. Label and freeze up to 3 months.

5. Remove bay leaf from Mushroom Beef Stew. Before serving, taste, and season again with salt and pepper.

A. SIRLOIN TIP WITH MUSTARD-APPLE SAUCE
SERVES 2

Sweet apple jelly, tangy Dijon mustard, and white wine combine to give this sirloin tip a snappy taste.

Half of a 2-pound sirloin tip
Salt and freshly ground black pepper, to
    taste
2 cloves garlic, minced, or 1 teaspoon bottled
    minced garlic
1 small onion, roughly chopped
1/3 cup white wine
1/3 cup apple juice
3 tablespoons apple jelly
1 tablespoon Dijon mustard
1/2 teaspoon curry powder

1. Insert liner into the slow cooker, fully opening the bag and draping the excess over the sides.

2. Add sirloin to the bottom of the liner. Season with salt and pepper.

3. Top sirloin with garlic and onion.

4. Stir together wine, apple juice, apple jelly, mustard, and curry powder in a small bowl. Pour over sirloin.

5. Fold the top of the bag over to one side and push ingredients at bottom of liner over to create room for the second bag.

6. Follow directions for the second recipe.

B. SIRLOIN TIP WITH FALL VEGETABLES

SERVES 2

This hearty beef dish seasoned with thyme and rosemary is a one-pot meal with the parsnip, sweet potato, and carrots.

Half of a 2-pound sirloin tip
Salt and freshly ground black pepper, to taste
1 parsnip, peeled and diced
1 small sweet potato, peeled and diced
10 baby carrots, sliced
1/2 cup beef broth
2 tablespoon apple cider vinegar
1/2 teaspoon dried thyme
1/2 teaspoon dried rosemary

1. Insert liner into the remaining space in the slow cooker, fully opening the bag and draping the excess over the sides.

2. Add sirloin to the bottom of the liner. Season with salt and pepper.

3. Top sirloin with parsnip, sweet potato, and carrots.

4. Stir together broth, vinegar, thyme, and rosemary in a small bowl. Pour over sirloin.

5. Fold the top of the bag over to the opposite side of the first bag and nestle the ingredients of both bags so that they are sharing the space evenly.

TO COMPLETE THE RECIPES:

1. Each closed liner should be draping away from the other, extending over the sides of the slow cooker.

2. Cover and cook on LOW for 5 hours.

3. Move two shallow serving dishes or bowls next to the slow cooker. Remove cover and using pot holders or oven mitts, carefully open each liner and remove the solids with a slotted spoon or tongs to its own serving bowl. Still using a pot holder, gather the top of the first liner, carefully lift the bag from the slow cooker and move over its serving bowl. Cut a corner off the bottom of the bag, large enough to allow the remaining contents of the bag to be released into the bowl. Discard the liner. Repeat with the second liner.

4. Allow the recipe not being served to cool, and package in a resealable plastic freezer bag or freezer container. Label and freeze up to 3 months.

5. Before serving, taste, and season again with salt and pepper.

A. EAT-IN CHINESE BEEF

SERVES 2

Plan ahead and you'll cancel your Chinese take-out. The only thing you'll miss will be the fortune cookies!

Half of a 2-pound sirloin tip, cut into 1-inch cubes
Freshly ground black pepper, to taste
1 small onion, sliced
1 clove garlic, minced, or ½ teaspoon bottled minced garlic
2 tablespoons hoisin sauce
3 tablespoons soy sauce
1 teaspoon dark sesame oil
1 teaspoon Chinese five-spice powder
2 green onions, sliced, white and green parts,
Crushed red pepper flakes, optional

1. Insert liner into the slow cooker, fully opening the bag and draping the excess over the sides.

2. Add sirloin to the bottom of the liner. Season with pepper.

3. Top sirloin with onion and garlic.

4. Stir together hoisin sauce, soy sauce, sesame oil, and five-spice powder in a small bowl. Pour over sirloin.

5. Reserve green onions and crushed red pepper flakes to top finished dish for serving.

6. Fold the top of the bag over to one side and push ingredients at bottom of liner over to create room for the second bag.

7. Follow directions for the second recipe.

continued >

B. SIRLOIN TIP WITH RED BELL PEPPERS
SERVES 2

Red bell peppers brighten up any dish and here they enliven this roast. Nice to pick up a little extra vitamin C and antioxidants with your dinner, too.

Half of a 2-pound sirloin tip, cut into 1-inch cubes

Salt and freshly ground black pepper, to taste

1 small onion, sliced

2 cloves garlic, minced, or 1 teaspoon bottled minced garlic

10 baby carrots, sliced

1 red bell pepper, cored, seeded, and sliced

1/2 cup beef broth

2 tablespoons tomato paste

4 sprigs fresh rosemary, divided

1. Insert liner into the remaining space in the slow cooker, fully opening the bag and draping the excess over the sides.

2. Add sirloin to the bottom of the liner. Season with salt and pepper.

3. Top sirloin with onion, garlic, carrots, and bell pepper.

4. Stir together beef broth and tomato paste in a small bowl. Pour over sirloin and vegetables.

5. Top with 2 sprigs fresh rosemary.

6. Reserve remaining rosemary to top finished dish for serving.

7. Fold the top of the bag over to the opposite side of the first bag and nestle the ingredients of both bags so that they are sharing the space evenly.

TO COMPLETE THE RECIPES:

1. Each closed liner should be draping away from the other, extending over the sides of the slow cooker.

2. Cover and cook on LOW for 6 hours.

3. Move two shallow serving dishes or bowls next to the slow cooker. Remove cover and using pot holders or oven mitts, carefully open each liner and remove the solids with a slotted spoon or tongs to its own serving bowl. Still using a pot holder, gather the top of the first liner, carefully lift the bag from the slow cooker and move over its serving bowl. Cut a corner off the bottom of the bag, large enough to allow the remaining contents of the bag to be released into the bowl. Discard the liner. Repeat with the second liner.

4. Allow the recipe not being served to cool, and package in a resealable plastic freezer bag or freezer container. Label and freeze up to 3 months.

5. Before serving, taste, and season again with salt and pepper. Top the Eat-In Chinese Beef with reserved green onion and crushed red pepper before serving. Top the Sirloin Tip with Red Bell Peppers with the reserved rosemary before serving.

PORK

Pork tenderloin was born for the slow cooker. It readily takes on the flavors of every cuisine, making it an incredibly versatile meat.

A. CHERRY BALSAMIC PORK

SERVES 2

Pork tenderloin was born for slow cooking, and using jams or preserves is a great trick for producing a quick sauce. This dish cries out for mashed potatoes.

½ **pound pork tenderloin (½ of a small tenderloin)**

Salt and freshly ground black pepper, to taste

1 teaspoon chopped fresh sage, or ¼ teaspoon dried sage

1 tablespoon minced shallot, or finely diced onion

¼ teaspoon ground cinnamon

¼ teaspoon ground nutmeg

¼ cup cherry preserves

½ cup fresh or frozen pitted dark cherries, defrosted

2 tablespoons balsamic vinegar

1. Insert liner into the slow cooker, fully opening the bag and draping the excess over the sides.

2. Add pork to the bottom of the liner. Season with salt and pepper.

3. Top with sage.

4. Stir together shallot, cinnamon, nutmeg, and cherry preserves in a small bowl.

5. Add cherries to shallot mixture and stir in vinegar. Pour over pork.

6. Fold the top of the bag over to one side and push ingredients at bottom of liner over to create room for the second bag.

7. Follow directions for the second recipe.

continued >

B. GARLIC CITRUS PORK
SERVES 2

Pork and citrus is a classic combination, and this tender pork will melt in your mouth.

---

1 teaspoon freshly ground black pepper
3 tablespoons lemon juice
2 cloves garlic, minced
1 tablespoon honey
1/2 pound pork tenderloin (1/2 of a small tenderloin)
1 lime, sliced
1/2 orange, sliced

1. Insert liner into the remaining space in the slow cooker, fully opening the bag and draping the excess over the sides.

2. Stir together pepper, lemon juice, garlic, and honey in a small bowl.

3. Rub onto pork. Add pork to bottom of liner.

4. Top pork with lime and orange slices.

5. Fold the top of the bag over to the opposite side of the first bag and nestle the ingredients of both bags so that they are sharing the space evenly.

TO COMPLETE THE RECIPES:

1. Each closed liner should be draping away from the other, extending over the sides of the slow cooker.

2. Cover and cook on LOW for 5 hours.

3. Move two shallow serving dishes or bowls next to the slow cooker. Remove cover and using pot holders or oven mitts, carefully open each liner and remove the solids with a slotted spoon or tongs to its own serving bowl. Still using a pot holder, gather the top of the first liner, carefully lift the bag from the slow

cooker and move over its serving bowl. Cut a corner off the bottom of the bag, large enough to allow the remaining contents of the bag to be released into the bowl. Discard the liner. Repeat with the second liner.

4. Allow the recipe not being served to cool, and package in a resealable plastic freezer bag or freezer container. Label and freeze up to 3 months.

5. Before serving, taste, and season again with salt and pepper.

A. PARMESAN-CRUSTED PORK TENDERLOIN

SERVES 2

The Parmesan cheese covers the pork to seal in the garlic and herbs.

½ pound pork tenderloin (½ of small tenderloin)

Salt and freshly ground black pepper, to taste

¼ cup honey

1 tablespoon soy sauce

1 tablespoon dried basil or chives

1 clove garlic, minced or ½ teaspoon bottled minced garlic

1 tablespoon olive oil

⅓ cup shredded or grated Parmesan cheese

1. Insert liner into the slow cooker, fully opening the bag and draping the excess over the sides.

2. Add pork to the bottom of the liner. Season with salt and pepper.

3. Stir together honey, soy sauce, dried basil or chives, garlic, and olive oil in a small bowl. Pour over pork.

4. Top pork with Parmesan cheese.

5. Fold the top of the bag over to one side and push ingredients at bottom of liner over to create room for the second bag.

6. Follow directions for the second recipe.

continued >

B. BBQ PORK TENDERLOIN
SERVES 2

In a pinch you can toss the tenderloin in the slow cooker with a bottle of your favorite sauce. Chop pork to serve in sandwich buns.

½ **pound pork tenderloin (½ of small tenderloin)**
Salt and freshly ground black pepper, to taste
½ **cup ketchup**
2 tablespoons light or dark brown sugar
1 tablespoon vinegar
1 teaspoon Dijon mustard
1 tablespoon soy sauce
½ **teaspoon chili powder**
1 clove garlic, minced, or ½ **teaspoon bottled minced garlic**
½ **teaspoon onion powder**

1. Insert liner into the remaining space in the slow cooker, fully opening the bag and draping the excess over the sides.

2. Add pork to the bottom of the liner. Season with salt and pepper.

3. Stir together ketchup, brown sugar, vinegar, Dijon mustard, soy sauce, chili powder, garlic, and onion powder in a small bowl. Pour over pork.

4. Fold the top of the bag over to the opposite side of the first bag and nestle the ingredients of both bags so that they are sharing the space evenly.

TO COMPLETE THE RECIPES:

1. Each closed liner should be draping away from the other, extending over the sides of the slow cooker.

2. Cover and cook on LOW for 6 hours.

3. Move two shallow serving dishes or bowls next to the slow cooker. Remove cover and using pot holders or oven mitts, carefully open each liner and remove the solids with a slotted spoon or tongs to its own serving bowl. Still using a pot holder, gather the top of the first liner, carefully lift the bag from the slow cooker and move over its serving bowl. Cut a corner off the bottom of the bag, large enough to allow the remaining contents of the bag to be released into the bowl. Discard the liner. Repeat with the second liner.

4. Allow the recipe not being served to cool, and package in a resealable plastic freezer bag or freezer container. Label and freeze up to 3 months.

5. Before serving, taste, and season again with salt and pepper.

A. BRUNSWICK STEW

SERVES 2

You'll know what to do with the rest of the beer once you taste this dish.

½ **pound pork tenderloin (½ of small tenderloin), cut into 1-inch cubes**
Salt and freshly ground black pepper, to taste
½ **cup frozen lima beans**
½ **cup frozen corn kernels**
1 small onion, chopped
1 (14½-ounce) can diced tomatoes, drained
⅓ **cup dark beer**
3 tablespoons ketchup
1 tablespoon cider vinegar
1 tablespoon brown sugar
1 tablespoon Worcestershire sauce
1 teaspoon smoky paprika
2 cloves garlic, minced, or 1 teaspoon bottled minced garlic
Bottled hot pepper sauce

1. Insert liner into the slow cooker, fully opening the bag and draping the excess over the sides.

2. Add pork to the bottom of the liner. Season with salt and pepper.

3. Top pork with lima beans, corn, and onion.

4. Stir together the tomatoes, beer, ketchup, vinegar, brown sugar, Worcestershire sauce, paprika, and garlic in a medium bowl. Pour over pork and vegetables.

5. Reserve hot sauce to season finished dish for serving.

6. Fold the top of the bag over to one side and push ingredients at bottom of liner over to create room for the second bag.

7. Follow directions for the second recipe.

B. SATAY-STYLE PORK STEW

SERVES 2

This dish has the flavor of popular grilled satay dishes, but using the slow cooker and a peanut butter-ginger spread. This dish is equally as good prepared with chicken.

½ **pound pork tenderloin (½ of a small tenderloin), cut into 1-inch cubes**
2 **tablespoons creamy peanut butter**
1 **teaspoon freshly grated ginger**
½ **red bell pepper, sliced**
1 **small red onion, sliced**
¼ **cup chunky salsa**
2 **teaspoons lime juice**
¼ **cup peanuts, chopped**
2 **green onions, sliced in 1-inch pieces, using some of the green parts**

1. Insert liner into the remaining space in the slow cooker, fully opening the bag and draping the excess over the sides.

2. Stir together pork, peanut butter, and ginger in a medium bowl to coat pork evenly with peanut butter.

3. Add red bell pepper, onion, salsa, and lime juice to pork, stirring well to mix.

4. Add pork mixture to the bottom of the liner.

5. Reserve peanuts and green onions to top finished dish for serving.

6. Fold the top of the bag over to the opposite side of the first bag and nestle the ingredients of both bags so that they are sharing the space evenly.

TO COMPLETE THE RECIPES:

1. Each closed liner should be draping away from the other, extending over the sides of the slow cooker.

2. Cover and cook on HIGH for 4½ hours.

3. Move two shallow serving dishes or bowls next to the slow cooker. Remove cover and using pot holders or oven mitts, carefully open each liner and remove the solids with a slotted spoon or tongs to its own serving bowl. Still using a pot holder, gather the top of the first liner, carefully lift the bag from the slow cooker and move over its serving bowl. Cut a corner

off the bottom of the bag, large enough to allow the remaining contents of the bag to be released into the bowl. Discard the liner. Repeat with the second liner.

4. Allow the recipe not being served to cool, and package in a resealable plastic freezer bag or freezer container. Label and freeze up to 3 months.

5. Before serving, taste, and season again with salt and pepper. Season Brunswick Stew with reserved hot sauce. Top Satay-Style Pork Stew with reserved peanuts and green onions.

A. PORK STEW WITH GREMOLATA

SERVES 2

Gremolata is a traditional Italian topping of chopped parsley, garlic, and lemon zest used in a variety of ways. Here it gives this dish a zing. You'll be tempted to skip it, but don't. It really makes this dish outstanding.

½ **pound pork tenderloin (½ of small tenderloin), cut into 1-inch cubes**
Salt and freshly ground black pepper, to taste
1 small onion, diced
10 baby carrots, chopped
1 (14½-ounce) can diced tomatoes
¼ cup white wine
¼ cup beef broth
1 clove garlic, minced, or ½ teaspoon bottled minced garlic
3 –4 sprigs fresh rosemary
¼ cup chopped fresh parsley
1 teaspoon lemon zest
2 cloves garlic, minced, or 1 teaspoon bottled minced garlic

1. Insert liner into the slow cooker, fully opening the bag and draping the excess over the sides.

2. Add pork to the bottom of the liner. Season with salt and pepper.

3. Top pork with onion and carrots.

4. Stir together tomatoes, white wine, broth, and garlic in a medium bowl. Pour over pork and vegetables.

5. Top pork with rosemary sprigs.

6. Reserve parsley, lemon zest, and garlic to top finished dish for serving.

7. Fold the top of the bag over to one side and push ingredients at bottom of liner over to create room for the second bag.

8. Follow directions for the second recipe.

continued >

B. ISLAND PORK CHILI

SERVES 2

This tastes like comfort food to me. Cilantro lovers may increase the amount, or if that's not your cup of tea, substitute Italian parsley. In a pinch, canned peaches substitute for mangos. Serve over rice.

½ pound pork tenderloin (½ of small tenderloin), cut into ½-inch cubes
Salt and freshly ground black pepper, to taste
1 (14½-ounce) can diced tomatoes, drained
¼ cup frozen corn kernels
½ cup black beans, rinsed and drained
½ teaspoon cumin
½ teaspoon chili powder
1 mango, diced, divided
⅓ cup chopped fresh cilantro, divided

1. Insert liner into the remaining space in the slow cooker, fully opening the bag and draping the excess over the sides.

2. Add pork to the bottom of the liner. Season with salt and pepper.

4. Stir together tomatoes, corn, black beans, cumin, and chili powder in a medium bowl. Pour over pork.

5. Top with half of the mango.

6. Fold the top of the bag over to the opposite side of the first bag and nestle the ingredients of both bags so that they are sharing the space evenly.

7. Reserve second half of mango and cilantro to top finished dish before serving.

TO COMPLETE THE RECIPES:

1. Each closed liner should be draping away from the other, extending over the sides of the slow cooker.

2. Cover and cook on LOW for 6 hours.

3. Move two shallow serving dishes or bowls next to the slow cooker. Remove cover and using pot holders or oven mitts, carefully open each liner and remove the solids with a slotted spoon or tongs to its own serving bowl. Still using a pot holder, gather the top of the first liner, carefully lift the bag from the slow cooker and move over its serving bowl. Cut a corner off the bottom of the bag, large enough to allow the remaining contents of the bag to be released into the bowl. Discard the liner. Repeat with the second liner.

4. Allow the recipe not being served to cool, and package in a resealable plastic freezer bag or freezer container. Label and freeze up to 3 months.

5. Before serving, taste, and season again with salt and pepper. Top Pork Stew with Gremolata with the reserved parsley, lemon zest and garlic before serving. Top Island Pork Stew with mango and cilantro before serving.

A. CUMIN-LIME PORK
SERVES 2

The onions just melt in this superb dish.

½ pound pork tenderloin (½ of small tenderloin)

Salt and freshly ground black pepper, to taste

2 teaspoons grated lime rind, no white attached, reserved

3 tablespoons lime juice

¼ cup orange juice

½ teaspoon dried oregano

½ teaspoon ground cumin

2 cloves garlic, minced, or 1 teaspoon bottled minced garlic

1 small onion, thinly sliced

1. Insert liner into the slow cooker, fully opening the bag and draping the excess over the sides.

2. Add pork to the bottom of the liner. Season with salt and pepper.

3. Reserve lime rind to top finished dish for serving.

4. Stir together lime juice, orange juice, oregano, cumin, and garlic in a small bowl. Pour over pork.

5. Top pork with onion slices.

6. Fold the top of the bag over to one side and push ingredients at bottom of liner over to create room for the second bag.

7. Follow directions for the second recipe.

B. RED PEPPER PORK

SERVES 2

This vivid red dish is hearty and satisfying. I serve it with rice. Roasted red peppers are available in jars and are a real time saver in the kitchen. Rinse and dry them before adding to the recipe.

½ **pound pork tenderloin (½ of small tenderloin)**

Salt and freshly ground black pepper, to taste

1 roasted red bell pepper, finely diced

2 teaspoons olive oil

1 teaspoon honey

1. Insert liner into the remaining space in the slow cooker, fully opening the bag and draping the excess over the sides.

2. Add pork to the bottom of the liner. Season with salt and pepper.

3. Stir together bell pepper, olive oil, and honey in a small bowl, mashing the bell pepper as needed to make a thick sauce. Pour over pork.

4. Fold the top of the bag over to the opposite side of the first bag and nestle the ingredients of both bags so that they are sharing the space evenly.

TO COMPLETE THE RECIPES:

1. Each closed liner should be draping away from the other, extending over the sides of the slow cooker.

2. Cover and cook on High for 4 hours.

3. Move two shallow serving dishes or bowls next to the slow cooker. Remove cover and using pot holders or oven mitts, carefully open each liner and remove the solids with a slotted spoon or tongs to its own serving bowl. Still using a pot holder, gather the top of the first liner, carefully lift the bag from the slow cooker and move over its serving bowl. Cut a corner

off the bottom of the bag, large enough to allow the remaining contents of the bag to be released into the bowl. Discard the liner. Repeat with the second liner.

4. Allow the recipe not being served to cool, and package in a resealable plastic freezer bag or freezer container. Label and freeze up to 3 months.

5. Before serving, taste, and season again with salt and pepper. Top the Cumin-Lime Pork with reserved lime zest before serving.

A. HERB AND LEMON PORK

SERVES 2

This pork is a light dish that's tangy and moist. Serve with bread to sop up the juices.

½ **pound pork tenderloin (**½ **of small tenderloin)**
¼ **cup chicken broth**
Salt and freshly ground black pepper, to taste
1 lemon, halved
1 tablespoon dried tarragon
1 tablespoon dried rosemary

1. Insert liner into the slow cooker, fully opening the bag and draping the excess over the sides.

2. Add pork to the bottom of the liner. Pour chicken broth over pork. Season with salt and pepper.

3. Squeeze half a lemon over pork, reserving second half for topping finished dish for serving.

4. Sprinkle pork with tarragon and rosemary.

5. Fold the top of the bag over to one side and push ingredients at bottom of liner over to create room for the second bag.

6. Follow directions for the second recipe.

B. GINGER GARLIC PORK

SERVES 2

This lovely dish has just a hint of sweetness. Substitute Italian parsley for the cilantro if you must.

½ pound pork tenderloin (½ of small tenderloin)
Salt and freshly ground black pepper, to taste
1 teaspoon apple cider vinegar
2 cloves garlic, minced, or 1 teaspoon bottled minced garlic
1 teaspoon freshly grated ginger
1 teaspoon olive oil
¼ cup beef stock
2 tablespoons chopped fresh cilantro
1 small onion, diced
2 green onions, sliced, white and green parts

1. Insert liner into the remaining space in the slow cooker, fully opening the bag and draping the excess over the sides.

2. Add pork to the bottom of the liner. Season with salt and pepper.

3. Stir together vinegar, garlic, ginger, and olive oil in a small bowl. Add beef stock and whisk to form a marinade. Pour over pork.

4. Top pork with cilantro and diced onion.

5. Reserve green onions to top finished dish for serving.

6. Fold the top of the bag over to the opposite side of the first bag and nestle the ingredients of both bags so that they are sharing the space evenly.

TO COMPLETE THE RECIPES:

1. Each closed liner should be draping away from the other, extending over the sides of the slow cooker.

2. Cover and cook on HIGH for 4 hours.

3. Move two shallow serving dishes or bowls next to the slow cooker. Remove cover and using pot holders or oven mitts, carefully open each liner and remove the solids with a slotted spoon or tongs to its own serving bowl. Still using a pot holder, gather the top of the first liner, carefully lift the bag from the slow cooker and move over its serving bowl. Cut a corner off the bottom of the bag, large enough to allow the remaining contents of the bag to be released into the bowl. Discard the liner. Repeat with the second liner.

4. Allow the recipe not being served to cool, and package in a resealable plastic freezer bag or freezer container. Label and freeze up to 3 months.

5. Before serving, taste, and season again with salt and pepper. Squeeze remaining ½ lemon over Herb and Lemon Pork. Top the Ginger Garlic Pork with green onions before serving.

A. SAGED PORK WITH FIGS

SERVES 2

For a perfect meal, serve this moist, fruity pork dish with rice or noodles and a side of grilled asparagus.

½ **pound pork tenderloin (**½ **of a small tenderloin), cut into** ½**-inch slices**

Salt and freshly ground black pepper, to taste

1 tablespoon minced shallot, or minced onion

½ **cup chicken broth**

4 fresh sage leaves, chopped, divided, or ¼ **teaspoon dried sage**

2 tablespoons fig jam or preserves

10 dried figs

1. Insert liner into the slow cooker, fully opening the bag and draping the excess over the sides.

2. Add pork to bottom of liner with slices slightly overlapping. Season with salt and pepper.

3. Top with shallot or onion.

4. Stir together chicken broth, 2 sage leaves, fig jam, and figs in a small bowl. Pour over pork.

5. Reserve remaining sage to top finished dish for serving.

6. Fold the top of the bag over to one side and push ingredients at bottom of liner over to create room for the second bag.

7. Follow directions for the second recipe.

continued >

B. PORK DIJON WITH FENNEL AND VEGETABLES

SERVES 2

Fennel retains some of its crunch, even after cooking. Here it highlights the sweet potato and parsnip for a one-pot dish.

½ **pound pork tenderloin (½ of a small tenderloin), cut into 1-inch cubes**
1 **tablespoon Dijon mustard**
1 **clove garlic, minced**
Salt and freshly ground black pepper, to taste
1 **small sweet potato, peeled and diced**
1 **small parsnip, peeled and diced**
1 **small onion, sliced**
½ **fennel bulb, sliced**
½ **cup chicken broth**

1. Insert liner into the remaining space in the slow cooker, fully opening the bag and draping the excess over the sides.

2. Toss pork, mustard, and garlic together in a small bowl. Add to the bottom of the liner. Season with salt and pepper.

3. Add sweet potato, parsnip, onion, and fennel on top of pork.

4. Pour chicken broth over pork and vegetables.

5. Fold the top of the bag over to the opposite side of the first bag and nestle the ingredients of both bags so that they are sharing the space evenly.

TO COMPLETE THE RECIPES:

1. Each closed liner should be draping away from the other, extending over the sides of the slow cooker.

2. Cover and cook on LOW for 5 hours.

3. Move two shallow serving dishes or bowls next to the slow cooker. Remove cover and using pot holders or oven mitts, carefully open each liner and remove the solids with a slotted spoon or tongs to its own serving bowl. Still using a pot holder, gather the top of the first liner, carefully lift the bag from the slow cooker and move over its serving bowl. Cut a corner off the bottom of the bag, large enough to allow the remaining contents of the bag to be released into the bowl. Discard the liner. Repeat with the second liner.

4. Allow the recipe not being served to cool, and package in a resealable plastic freezer bag or freezer container. Label and freeze up to 3 months.

5. Before serving, taste, and season again with salt and pepper. Top Saged Pork with Figs with chopped fresh sage, if desired.

A. GARAM MASALA PORK
SERVES 2

Garam masala is a traditional spice mixture used in Indian cooking. There are as many different combinations as there are cooks, but most contain at least cumin, coriander, cinnamon, cardamom, and pepper. Serve this dish over rice.

½ pound pork tenderloin (½ of small tenderloin), cut into 1-inch cubes
Salt and freshly ground pepper, to taste
3 cloves garlic, minced, or 1½ teaspoons bottled minced garlic
1 tablespoon freshly grated ginger or 1 teaspoon ground ginger
½ teaspoon chili powder
½ teaspoon garam masala

1. Insert liner into the slow cooker, fully opening the bag and draping the excess over the sides.

2. Place pork in a medium-sized bowl. Season with salt and pepper.

3. Stir garlic, ginger, chili powder, and garam masala into a paste in a small bowl.

4. Rub the paste into the pork, coating the pork evenly. Move pork to the bottom of the liner.

5. Fold the top of the bag over to one side and push ingredients at bottom of liner over to create room for the second bag.

6. Follow directions for the second recipe.

continued >

B. PORK TENDERLOIN WITH GINGER-MANGO SAUCE

SERVES 2

Mango, ginger, and pork are a mellow, soothing trio. Serve this dish over rice.

½ pound pork tenderloin (½ of small tenderloin)
Salt and freshly ground black pepper, to taste
2 tablespoons dry sherry
2 tablespoons light or dark brown sugar
2 teaspoons freshly grated ginger
1 teaspoon chopped fresh thyme
1 teaspoon chopped fresh rosemary
1 medium mango, peeled and sliced, half diced, divided

1. Insert liner into the remaining space in the slow cooker, fully opening the bag and draping the excess over the sides.

2. Add the pork to the bottom of the liner. Season with salt and pepper.

3. Stir together sherry, brown sugar, ginger, thyme, rosemary, and diced mango in a small bowl. Pour over pork.

4. Reserve remaining mango to top finished dish for serving.

5. Fold the top of the bag over to the opposite side of the first bag and nestle the ingredients of both bags so that they are sharing the space evenly.

TO COMPLETE THE RECIPES:

1. Each closed liner should be draping away from the other, extending over the sides of the slow cooker.

2. Cover and cook on LOW for 5 hours.

3. Move two shallow serving dishes or bowls next to the slow cooker. Remove cover and using pot holders or oven mitts, carefully open each liner and remove the solids with a slotted spoon or tongs to its own serving bowl. Still using a pot holder, gather the top of the first liner, carefully lift the bag from the slow cooker and move over its serving bowl. Cut a corner off the bottom of the bag, large enough to allow the remaining contents of the bag to be released into the bowl. Discard the liner. Repeat with the second liner.

4. Allow the recipe not being served to cool, and package in a resealable plastic freezer bag or freezer container. Label and freeze up to 3 months.

5. Before serving, taste, and season again with salt and pepper. Top the Pork Tenderloin with Ginger-Mango Sauce with reserved mango.

A. PORK TENDERLOIN WITH CABBAGE
SERVES 2

This dish from my childhood was always served with a side of warm applesauce. Old habits die hard. Do try it. Substitute a slaw mix for the cabbage, omitting the carrot and cabbage below, if desired.

½ pound pork tenderloin (½ of a small tenderloin)
¼ cup water
Salt and freshly ground pepper, to taste
1 teaspoon cumin
1 teaspoon garlic powder
1 teaspoon dried basil
1 small carrot, chopped
1 small onion, chopped
½ (8-ounce) bag shredded cabbage
½ teaspoon fennel seed

1. Insert liner into the slow cooker, fully opening the bag and draping the excess over the sides.

2. Add pork to the bottom of the liner. Pour water over pork.

3. Season with salt, pepper, cumin, garlic, and basil.

4. Top pork with carrot, onion, cabbage, and fennel seed.

5. Fold the top of the bag over to one side and push ingredients at bottom of liner over to create room for the second bag.

6. Follow directions for the second recipe.

B. JERK PORK TENDERLOIN

SERVES 2

Serve this spicy and fun pork dish with yellow or white rice. If pressed for time, a prepared jerk seasoning may be substituted for the spices.

1 cup beef broth
1 teaspoon onion powder
1 teaspoon garlic powder
1 teaspoon crushed red pepper flakes
¼ teaspoon allspice
¼ teaspoon ground cinnamon
¼ teaspoon ground ginger
⅛ teaspoon ground cloves
½ pound pork tenderloin (½ of a small tenderloin)

1. Insert liner into the remaining space in the slow cooker, fully opening the bag and draping the excess over the sides.

2. Add beef broth to the bottom of the liner.

3. Stir together onion powder, garlic powder, crushed red pepper, allspice, cinnamon, ginger, and cloves in a small bowl. Rub spice mixture into pork.

4. Place pork in the bottom of the liner.

5. Fold the top of the bag over to the opposite side of the first bag and nestle the ingredients of both bags so that they are sharing the space evenly.

TO COMPLETE THE RECIPES:

1. Each closed liner should be draping away from the other, extending over the sides of the slow cooker.

2. Cover and cook on LOW for 6 hours.

3. Move two shallow serving dishes or bowls next to the slow cooker. Remove cover and using pot holders or oven mitts, carefully open each liner and remove the solids with a slotted spoon or tongs to its own serving bowl. Still using a pot holder, gather the top of the first liner, carefully lift the bag from the slow cooker and move over its serving bowl. Cut a corner off the bottom of the bag, large enough to allow the remaining contents of the bag to be released into the bowl. Discard the liner. Repeat with the second liner.

4. Allow the recipe not being served to cool, and package in a resealable plastic freezer bag or freezer container. Label and freeze up to 3 months.

5. Before serving, taste, and season again with salt and pepper.

A. CRANBERRY-ORANGE PORK CHOPS

SERVES 2

Blade pork chops are a little less expensive that other pork cuts, and are a little tougher. Your slow cooker comes to the rescue to make them perfectly juicy and tender.

2 (7-ounce) bone-in, blade-cut pork chops
Salt and freshly ground black pepper, to taste
1 small onion, diced
1/3 cup chicken broth
2 tablespoons grated orange zest, no white attached, divided
2 tablespoons orange juice
1 tablespoon lemon juice
1 tablespoon maple syrup
1/4 cup dried cranberries
6–8 sprigs fresh thyme, divided

1. Insert liner into the slow cooker, fully opening the bag and draping the excess over the sides.

2. Add pork chops to the bottom of the liner. Season with salt and pepper.

3. Top the pork chops with onion.

4. Stir together broth, 1 tablespoon orange zest, orange juice, lemon juice, syrup, and cranberries in a small bowl. Pour over pork chops.

5. Top pork chops with 4 sprigs fresh thyme.

6. Reserve remaining orange zest and thyme sprigs to top finished dish for serving.

7. Fold the top of the bag over to one side and push ingredients at bottom of liner over to create room for the second bag.

8. Follow directions for the second recipe.

B. ASIAN PORK CHOPS
SERVES 2

I've omitted the salt here, as the soy sauce provides plenty and you won't miss it. These chops are superb and call for a side dish of rice.

2 (7-ounce) bone-in, blade-cut pork chops
Freshly ground black pepper, to taste
2 tablespoons soy sauce
1 tablespoon brown sugar
1 tablespoon ketchup
¼ teaspoon ground ginger
1 clove garlic, minced, or ½ teaspoon bottled
   minced garlic

1. Insert liner into the remaining space in the slow cooker, fully opening the bag and draping the excess over the sides.

2. Add pork chops to the bottom of the liner. Season with pepper.

3. Stir together soy sauce, brown sugar, ketchup, ginger, and garlic in a small bowl. Pour over pork chops.

4. Fold the top of the bag over to the opposite side of the first bag and nestle the ingredients of both bags so that they are sharing the space evenly.

TO COMPLETE THE RECIPES:

1. Each closed liner should be draping away from the other, extending over the sides of the slow cooker.

2. Cover and cook on LOW for 4 hours.

3. Move two shallow serving dishes or bowls next to the slow cooker. Remove cover and using pot holders or oven mitts, carefully open each liner and remove the solids with a slotted spoon or tongs to its own serving bowl. Still using a pot holder, gather the top of the first liner, carefully lift the bag from the slow cooker and move over its serving bowl. Cut a corner off the bottom of the bag, large enough to allow the remaining contents of the bag to be released into the bowl. Discard the liner. Repeat with the second liner.

4. Allow the recipe not being served to cool, and package in a resealable plastic freezer bag or freezer container. Label and freeze up to 3 months.

5. Before serving, taste, and season again with salt and pepper. Top the Cranberry-Orange Pork Chops with the remaining orange zest and thyme before serving.

A. PORK STEW WITH GREEN BEANS AND YELLOW SQUASH

SERVES 2

This pork stew has a slight bite from the hint of rum. Substitute bourbon or whiskey if you prefer, or omit. I serve this stew with a dark or multigrain bread.

1/2 **pound pork tenderloin (**1/2 **of a small tenderloin), cut into 1-inch cubes**
Salt and freshly ground black pepper, to taste
1 small onion, thinly sliced
2 cloves garlic, minced, or 1 teaspoon bottled minced garlic
2 tablespoons freshly grated ginger
1/2 **cup chicken broth**
3 tablespoons cider vinegar
2 tablespoons dark rum, optional
2 tablespoons light or dark brown sugar
1/2 **cup fresh or frozen green beans**
1 small yellow squash, sliced

1. Insert liner into the slow cooker, fully opening the bag and draping the excess over the sides.

2. Add pork to the bottom of the liner. Season with salt and pepper.

3. Top pork with onion slices.

4. Stir together garlic, ginger, chicken broth, vinegar, rum if using, and brown sugar in a small bowl. Pour over pork.

5. Top pork with green beans and squash.

6. Fold the top of the bag over to one side and push ingredients at bottom of liner over to create room for the second bag.

7. Follow directions for the second recipe.

continued >

B. SPICY PORK IN GARLIC SAUCE
SERVES 2

My favorite slow cooker ingredients in one dish. The hoisin sauce adds a depth of flavor and a little spice to the pork.

½ pound pork tenderloin (½ of a small
  tenderloin), cut into 1-inch cubes
1 tablespoon hoisin sauce
1 tablespoon freshly grated ginger
3 cloves garlic, minced, or 1½ teaspoons
  bottled minced garlic
3 tablespoons dry sherry
3 tablespoons soy sauce

1. Insert liner into the remaining space in the slow cooker, fully opening the bag and draping the excess over the sides.

2. Add pork to the bottom of liner.

3. Stir together hoisin sauce, ginger, garlic, dry sherry, and soy sauce in a small bowl. Pour over pork.

4. Fold the top of the bag over to the opposite side of the first bag and nestle the ingredients of both bags so that they are sharing the space evenly.

TO COMPLETE THE RECIPES:

1. Each closed liner should be draping away from the other, extending over the sides of the slow cooker.

2. Cover and cook on LOW for 5 hours.

3. Move two shallow serving dishes or bowls next to the slow cooker. Remove cover and using pot holders or oven mitts, carefully open each liner and remove the solids with a slotted spoon or tongs to its own serving bowl. Still using a pot holder, gather the top of the first liner, carefully lift the bag from the slow cooker and move over its serving bowl. Cut a corner off the bottom of the bag, large enough to allow the remaining contents of the bag to be released into the bowl. Discard the liner. Repeat with the second liner.

4. Allow the recipe not being served to cool, and package in a resealable plastic freezer bag or freezer container. Label and freeze up to 3 months.

5. Before serving, taste, and season again with salt and pepper.

LAMB

Lamb is a favorite of mine, but cooking a whole boneless leg of lamb isn't practical for just the two of us. However, one-pound packages of lamb stew meat are perfect for a double dinner. If unavailable, substitute with lamb blade chops.

A. MEDITERRANEAN LAMB AND OLIVE STEW

SERVES 2

Resist the temptation to use canned olives and try imported ones instead. Some grocery stores even have olive bars where you can bring home a variety to try. I like serving this dish with pita bread.

½ **pound lamb stew meat**
Salt and freshly ground black pepper, to taste
1 teaspoon herbes de Provence
¼ **cup red wine**
12–14 green olives
2 tablespoons chopped fresh parsley, or to taste
1 teaspoon grated lemon zest, no white attached

1. Insert liner into the slow cooker, fully opening the bag and draping the excess over the sides.

2. Add lamb to bottom of liner. Season with salt and pepper.

3. Sprinkle lamb with herbes de Provence.

4. Pour red wine over lamb. Top with green olives.

5. Reserve parsley and lemon zest to top finished dish for serving.

6. Fold the top of the bag over to one side and push ingredients at bottom of liner over to create room for the second bag.

7. Follow directions for the second recipe.

B. ROCKIN' MOROCCAN LAMB

SERVES 2

These robust flavors are delicious but not overpowering or heavy. The spices are heavenly.

½ pound lamb stew meat
Salt and freshly ground black pepper, to taste
1 small sweet potato, peeled and diced
10 baby carrots, chopped
½ cup pearl onions
¼ cup pitted whole dates, chopped
¼ teaspoon ground cumin
¼ teaspoon ground turmeric
¼ teaspoon ground cinnamon
½ teaspoon ground ginger
¼ cup chicken broth
2 teaspoon grated lemon zest, no white attached, divided
1 tablespoon lemon juice
2 teaspoons honey
1 clove garlic, minced

1. Insert liner into the remaining space in the slow cooker, fully opening the bag and draping the excess over the sides.

2. Add lamb to bottom of the liner. Season with salt and pepper.

3. Top lamb with sweet potato, carrots, onions, and dates.

4. Stir together cumin, turmeric, cinnamon, and ginger in a small bowl. Sprinkle over vegetables.

5. Whisk together chicken broth, 1 teaspoon lemon zest, lemon juice, honey, and garlic in a small bowl. Pour over vegetables.

6. Fold the top of the bag over to the opposite side of the first bag and nestle the ingredients of both bags so that they are sharing the space evenly.

7. Reserve second teaspoon of lemon zest to top finished dish for serving.

TO COMPLETE THE RECIPES:

1. Each closed liner should be draping away from the other, extending over the sides of the slow cooker.

2. Cover and cook on LOW for 5 hours.

3. Move two shallow serving dishes or bowls next to the slow cooker. Remove cover and using pot holders or oven mitts, carefully open each liner and remove the solids with a slotted spoon or tongs to its own serving bowl. Still using a pot holder, gather the top of the first liner, carefully lift the bag from the slow cooker and move over its serving bowl. Cut a corner off the bottom of the bag, large enough to allow the remaining contents of the bag to be released into the bowl. Discard the liner. Repeat with the second liner.

4. Allow the recipe not being served to cool, and package in a resealable plastic freezer bag or freezer container. Label and freeze up to 3 months.

5. Before serving, taste, and season again with salt and pepper. Top Mediterranean Lamb and Olive Stew with reserved parsley and lemon zest before serving. Top Rockin' Moroccan Lamb with reserved lemon zest.

A. ASIAN LAMB WITH EGGPLANT

SERVES 2

This spicy dish produces a great sauce, so serve over couscous or rice.

¹/₂ pound lamb stew meat
1 small eggplant, peeled and diced
1 tablespoon soy sauce
1 tablespoon rice vinegar
1 tablespoon sweet chili paste
1 tablespoon hoisin sauce
¹/₄ cup beef broth
1 teaspoon dark sesame oil
1 green onion, sliced into 1-inch pieces using some of the green parts

1. Insert liner into the slow cooker, fully opening the bag and draping the excess over the sides.

2. Add lamb to the bottom of the liner. Top with eggplant.

3. Whisk together soy sauce, rice vinegar, sweet chili paste, hoisin sauce, beef broth, and sesame oil in a small bowl. Pour over lamb.

4. Fold the top of the bag over to one side and push ingredients at bottom of liner over to create room for the second bag.

5. Reserve green onion to top finished dish for serving.

6. Follow directions for the second recipe.

continued >

B. MOROCCAN SPICED LAMB WITH DRIED FRUIT
SERVES 2

Don't let the fall colors of this dish fool you—it tastes lighter than it looks. Serve with couscous or rice.

½ pound lamb stew meat
Salt and freshly ground black pepper, to taste
1 small sweet potato, peeled and diced
1 small onion, minced
2 cloves garlic, minced, or 1 teaspoon bottled minced garlic
⅓ cup dried apricots, diced
1 teaspoon ground ginger
½ cup red wine
3 tablespoons sliced almonds

1. Insert liner into the remaining space in the slow cooker, fully opening the bag and draping the excess over the sides.

2. Add lamb to bottom of liner. Season with salt and pepper.

3. Top with sweet potato, onion, garlic, and apricots.

4. Stir ginger into wine in a small bowl. Pour over lamb and vegetables.

5. Reserve almonds to top finished dish for serving.

6. Fold the top of the bag over to the opposite side of the first bag and nestle the ingredients of both bags so that they are sharing the space evenly.

TO COMPLETE THE RECIPES:

1. Each closed liner should be draping away from the other, extending over the sides of the slow cooker.

2. Cover and cook on LOW for 5 hours.

3. Move two shallow serving dishes or bowls next to the slow cooker. Remove cover and using pot holders or oven mitts, carefully open each liner and remove the solids with a slotted spoon or tongs to its own serving bowl. Still using a pot holder, gather the top of the first liner, carefully lift the bag from the slow cooker and move over its serving bowl. Cut a corner off the bottom of the bag, large enough to allow the remaining contents of the bag to be released into the bowl. Discard the liner. Repeat with the second liner.

4. Allow the recipe not being served to cool, and package in a resealable plastic freezer bag or freezer container. Label and freeze up to 3 months.

5. Before serving, taste, and season again with salt and pepper. Top Asian Lamb with reserved green onion before serving. Top Moroccan Spiced Lamb with reserved sliced almonds before serving.

VEGETARIAN

Vegetarian dishes are a breeze in the slow cooker. Canned beans are an economical protein always at the ready in the pantry. Here are a few of my favorites. Experiment and create your own!

A. RED LENTIL STEW
SERVES 2

Lentils come in all colors and each has a slightly different taste. Red lentils taste a bit nutty and soften easily when cooking. Select your favorite rice to accompany this dish.

½ cup dried red lentils
10 baby carrots, sliced
1 small onion, finely chopped
1 clove garlic, minced, or ½ teaspoon bottled minced garlic
1 teaspoon freshly grated ginger
¼ teaspoon ground turmeric
¼ teaspoon ground cumin
¼ teaspoon ground coriander
¼ teaspoon ground cinnamon
½ cup water
½ of a (14-ounce) can coconut milk
1 small tomato, chopped
2 tablespoons chopped fresh cilantro, or to taste
Salt and freshly ground black pepper, to taste

1. Insert liner into the slow cooker, fully opening the bag and draping the excess over the sides.

2. Stir together lentils, carrots, and onion in a large bowl.

3. Stir together garlic, ginger, turmeric, cumin, coriander, and cinnamon in a small bowl. Pour over vegetables.

4. Pour water and coconut milk over vegetables, stirring well to mix. Add to the bottom of the liner.

5. Reserve tomato, cilantro, and salt and pepper to top finished dish for serving.

6. Fold the top of the bag over to one side and push ingredients at bottom of liner over to create room for the second bag.

7. Follow directions for the second recipe.

B. CAULIFLOWER AND BEAN CURRY

SERVES 2

Brown rice or mixed wild rice is a satisfying base for this vegetable curry.

1½ cups cauliflower florets
1 (15-ounce) can chickpeas, rinsed and drained
½ cup frozen or fresh cut green beans
1 small onion, chopped
10 baby carrots, sliced
½ cup vegetable broth
2 teaspoons curry powder
¼ cup chopped fresh basil, divided
½ of a (14-ounce) can coconut milk

1. Insert liner into the remaining space in the slow cooker, fully opening the bag and draping the excess over the sides.

2. Stir together cauliflower, chickpeas, green beans, onion, carrots, vegetable broth, curry powder and 3 tablespoons fresh basil in a medium bowl.

3. Add vegetable mixture to the bottom of the liner.

4. Reserve remaining basil and coconut milk to top finished dish for serving.

5. Fold the top of the bag over to the opposite side of the first bag and nestle the ingredients of both bags so that they are sharing the space evenly.

TO COMPLETE THE RECIPES:

1. Each closed liner should be draping away from the other, extending over the sides of the slow cooker.

2. Cover and cook on LOW for 4 hours.

3. Move two shallow serving dishes or bowls next to the slow cooker. Remove cover and using pot holders or oven mitts, carefully open each liner and remove the solids with a slotted spoon or tongs to its own serving bowl. Still using a pot holder, gather the top of the first liner, carefully lift the bag from the slow cooker and move over its serving bowl. Cut a corner off the bottom of the bag, large enough to allow the remaining contents of the bag to be released into the bowl. Discard the liner. Repeat with the second liner.

4. Allow the recipe not being served to cool, and package in a resealable plastic freezer bag or freezer container. Label and freeze up to 3 months.

5. Before serving, taste, and season again with salt and pepper. Top the Red Lentil Stew with tomato, cilantro, salt, and pepper before serving. Top the hot Cauliflower and Bean Curry with coconut milk and reserved basil before serving.

A. VEGETARIAN CHILI

SERVES 2

Chocolate and coffee are two secret weapons in the arsenal of chili makers. The cocoa powder here adds depth to the overall flavor. Be sure to rinse and drain the canned beans, as they are high in sodium unless the canning liquid is removed.

1 (15-ounce) can cannellini beans, rinsed and drained

1 (15-ounce) can black beans, rinsed and drained

1 (10-ounce) can diced tomatoes with green chile peppers

1/2 cup vegetable broth

2 teaspoons cocoa powder

2 teaspoons chili powder

1 teaspoon Cajun seasoning

2 teaspoons chopped fresh cilantro

1/2 cup shredded Mexican blend cheese, or cheddar cheese

1. Insert liner into the slow cooker, fully opening the bag and draping the excess over the sides.

2. Stir together cannellini beans, black beans, tomatoes with peppers, vegetable broth, cocoa powder, chili powder, and Cajun seasoning in a large bowl. Add to the bottom of the liner.

3. Reserve cilantro and cheese to top finished dish for serving.

4. Fold the top of the bag over to one side and push ingredients at bottom of liner over to create room for the second bag.

5. Follow directions for the second recipe.

B. WHITE BEAN AND RICE SOUP

SERVES 2

Canned beans are a pantry staple for me, so I can easily put together a soup or chili. The spinach adds color and nutrition to this dish, but if none is at hand, it is still a great dish.

1 (15½-ounce) can great northern beans, rinsed and drained
1 (8-ounce) can tomato sauce
½ teaspoon granulated sugar
1 small onion, chopped
1 clove garlic, minced, or ½ teaspoon bottled minced garlic
1 teaspoon dried tarragon
1½ cups vegetable broth
¼ cup uncooked, converted rice
1 (5-ounce) bag washed baby spinach
Salt and freshly ground black pepper, to taste
2 tablespoons shredded or grated Parmesan cheese

1. Insert liner into the remaining space in the slow cooker, fully opening the bag and draping the excess over the sides.

2. Stir together beans, tomato sauce, sugar, onion, garlic, tarragon, vegetable broth, and rice in a large bowl. Season with salt and pepper.

3. Add bean mixture to the bottom of the liner.

4. Reserve Parmesan cheese to top finished dish for serving.

5. Fold the top of the bag over to the opposite side of the first bag and nestle the ingredients of both bags so that they are sharing the space evenly.

TO COMPLETE THE RECIPES:

1. Each closed liner should be draping away from the other, extending over the sides of the slow cooker.

2. Cover and cook on LOW for 6 hours.

3. Move two shallow serving dishes or bowls next to the slow cooker. Remove cover and using pot holders or oven mitts, carefully open each liner and remove the solids with a slotted spoon or tongs to its own serving bowl. Still using a pot holder, gather the top of the first liner, carefully lift the bag from the slow cooker and move over its serving bowl. Cut a corner off the bottom of the bag, large enough to allow the remaining contents of the bag to be released into the bowl. Discard the liner. Repeat with the second liner.

4. Allow the recipe not being served to cool, and package in a resealable plastic freezer bag or freezer container. Label and freeze up to 3 months.

5. Before serving, taste, and season again with salt and pepper. Top Vegetarian Chili with cilantro and cheese before serving. Stir the spinach into the hot White Bean and Rice Soup and top with reserved Parmesan before serving.

A. RATATOUILLE

SERVES 2

Ratatouille is such a versatile dish. It's terrific over pasta, or makes a tasty side dish on its own with poultry and meats.

1 small eggplant, peeled and chopped
1 small zucchini, peeled and chopped
Salt and freshly ground black pepper, to taste
1 small onion, chopped
1 red bell pepper, seeded and chopped
4 ounces sliced, fresh mushrooms
2 small tomatoes, chopped
2 cloves garlic, minced, or 1 teaspoon bottled minced garlic
1 tablespoon balsamic vinegar
1 tablespoon olive oil
4–6 sprigs fresh thyme, divided

1. Insert liner into the slow cooker, fully opening the bag and draping the excess over the sides.

2. Add eggplant and zucchini to the bottom of the liner. Season with salt and pepper.

3. Top eggplant and zucchini with onion, bell pepper, mushrooms, tomatoes, and garlic.

4. Pour vinegar and oil over vegetables, stirring to mix.

5. Top vegetables with 4 sprigs of thyme.

6. Reserve remaining sprigs of thyme to top finished dish for serving, if desired.

7. Fold the top of the bag over to one side and push ingredients at bottom of liner over to create room for the second bag.

8. Follow directions for the second recipe.

B. APPLE AND VEGETABLE STEW

SERVES 2

Chop all of these vegetables in small dice in order that they will cook evenly and completely through. Your kitchen will smell like a perfect fall afternoon.

1 small sweet potato, peeled and diced
10 baby carrots, chopped
1 parsnip, peeled and diced
Salt and freshly ground black pepper, to taste
1/4 teaspoon ground cinnamon
1/2 teaspoon curry powder
1 Granny Smith or other tart apple, peeled and diced
1 small onion, diced
1/2 cup vegetable broth
1/4 cup chopped walnuts or pecans
Chopped fresh parsley

1. Insert liner into the remaining space in the slow cooker, fully opening the bag and draping the excess over the sides.

2. Add the sweet potato, carrots, and parsnip. Season with salt, pepper, cinnamon, and curry powder.

3. Top vegetables with apple and onion.

4. Pour broth over vegetable mixture, stirring well to mix.

5. Reserve nuts and parsley to top finished dish for serving.

6. Fold the top of the bag over to the opposite side of the first bag and nestle the ingredients of both bags so that they are sharing the space evenly.

TO COMPLETE THE RECIPES:

1. Each closed liner should be draping away from the other, extending over the sides of the slow cooker.

2. Cover and cook on LOW for 5 hours.

3. Move two shallow serving dishes or bowls next to the slow cooker. Remove cover and using pot holders or oven mitts, carefully open each liner and remove the solids with a slotted spoon or tongs to its own serving bowl. Still using a pot holder, gather the top of the first liner, carefully lift the bag from the slow cooker and move over its serving bowl. Cut a corner off the bottom of the bag, large enough to allow the remaining contents of the bag to be released into the bowl. Discard the liner. Repeat with the second liner.

4. Allow the recipe not being served to cool, and package in a resealable plastic freezer bag or freezer container. Label and freeze up to 3 months.

5. Before serving, taste, and season again with salt and pepper. Top the Ratatouille with reserved thyme before serving. Top the Apple and Vegetable Stew with nuts and parsley before serving.

INDEX

METRIC CONVERSION CHART

Volume Measurements		Weight Measurements		Temperature Conversion	
U.S.	**Metric**	**U.S.**	**Metric**	**Fahrenheit**	**Celsius**
1 teaspoon	5 ml	1/2 ounce	15 g	250	120
1 tablespoon	15 ml	1 ounce	30 g	300	150
1/4 cup	60 ml	3 ounces	90 g	325	160
1/3 cup	75 ml	4 ounces	115 g	350	180
1/2 cup	125 ml	8 ounces	225 g	375	190
2/3 cup	150 ml	12 ounces	350 g	400	200
3/4 cup	175 ml	1 pound	450 g	425	220
1 cup	250 ml	2 1/4 pounds	1 kg	450	230

ACKNOWLEDGMENTS

I owe a debt of gratitude to the incomparable Nathalie Dupree for her friendship, mentorship, and most of all, the idea for this book! I'm still loving our near thirty-year journey together and treasure your support.

My team is simply fabulous: photographer Rick McKee shot these taste-tempting photos (with the patience of a saint); talented food stylist Nan McCullough brought out the very best in my recipes (it's our second book together); Elise Garner is my right hand in times of crisis, exemplifying all you could want in an assistant; and Rebecca Battle, who has the most gentle and professional manner, was my double in thought, word, and deed when my energies had to be focused elsewhere during shooting.

My publishing team at Gibbs Smith gives me plenty of reasons why producing a book with a small publisher is such a pleasure. Deep thanks to my editor extraordinaire, Madge Baird. Thanks also to all of those who perform duties behind the scenes that when put together make a wonderful book that I'm proud to put my name on.

My family has enjoyed this journey with me and provides such love and support. Thank you to my husband, Cliff, and my children, Norman and Rachel.

ABOUT THE AUTHOR

James Beard Award winner and *Southern Living* magazine columnist Cynthia Graubart is passionate about bringing families together at the table. Her previous book is *Slow Cooking for Two: Basics, Techniques, Recipes.* She is the co-author of *Mastering the Art of Southern Cooking* (2013 James Beard Award) and *Southern Biscuits*, both with Nathalie Dupree. Her first book was *The One-Armed Cook: Quick and Easy Recipes, Smart Meal Plans, and Savvy Advice for New (and Not-So-New) Moms.* She travels the country as a speaker and cooking teacher, and is a member of the International Association of Culinary Professionals (IACP) and Les Dames d'Escoffier (LDEI) and has served on the board of the Atlanta Community Food Bank. She and her husband live in Atlanta, Georgia. Join Cynthia online at www.cynthiagraubart.com.